MARTIN KUMERT

# The Judgment Vacuum

*Why the AI era is producing smarter organizations and a generation unprepared to lead them—and what to do before it's too late*

First published 2026 by Symbiolabs Inc.

First edition

ISBN: 979-8-9955977-0-4

This book was professionally typeset on Reedsy.
Find out more at reedsy.com

# Contents


| | | |
|---|---|---|
| 1 | The Apprenticeship Chain | 1 |
| 2 | The Efficiency Trap | 9 |
| 3 | The AI Accelerant | 21 |
| 4 | The Generation Gap Nobody Talks About | 35 |
| 5 | When the Last Ones Retire | 50 |
| 6 | The Market Consequences | 63 |
| 7 | What Machines Cannot Inherit | 75 |
| 8 | The New Human Premium | 85 |
| 9 | Identity at Work | 101 |
| 10 | The New Leader's Job | 116 |
| 11 | Designing for Formation | 131 |
| 12 | The Adaptable Organization | 146 |
| 13 | The Choice | 161 |

# 1

# The Apprenticeship Chain



*Moment I — The Invisible Erosion*

*How judgment was always transmitted through friction, exposure, and gradual context accumulation — and why that system worked.*

There is a peculiar kind of knowledge that cannot be written down. It cannot be taught in a classroom, transferred in a briefing, or acquired by reading the right books. It has to be lived — slowly, imperfectly, and often uncomfortably — before it becomes part of how a person thinks. The philosopher Michael Polanyi gave this phenomenon a name in 1966: tacit knowledge. His formulation was precise — "we know more than we can tell" — and it pointed at something that every experienced practitioner already understood intuitively but had never quite found language for.[1] The knowledge that makes a surgeon's hands confident, that makes a seasoned investor's instincts reliable, that makes an experienced leader's judgment trustworthy in a crisis — none of it can be fully articulated. It is embedded in the person who holds it, inseparable from the history of how it was acquired.

Business judgment is this kind of knowledge. And for most of modern organizational history, we had a system for producing it. We just never called it a system.

We called it experience.

The word does not do justice to what was actually happening. "Experience" suggests passive accumulation — time served, years accrued. But the process was more deliberate than that, even when it felt accidental. It had a structure. It had a rhythm. It had, above all, a logic: each phase of a career was designed — not by plan but by necessity — to build the foundation for the next. Junior professionals did not simply complete tasks. They were, without always knowing it, being formed.

Think about what it actually meant to begin a career in a finance function thirty years ago. You were not managing dashboards. You were not automating reports. You were sitting close to the raw materials of organizational life — the invoices, the reconciliations, the month-end closes — and you were doing the work with your hands, slowly enough that you could not avoid understanding it.

A junior analyst in that environment did not merely produce outputs. He absorbed context. He learned, through repetition and proximity, that the revenue number on the P&L was not a fact — it was a consequence. It followed from decisions made six months earlier: which customers the sales team had prioritized, which payment terms had been negotiated, which projects had slipped and why. He learned that a variance in operating costs was not a problem to be reported but a signal to be read — because behind it was a story about a supplier relationship, a process breakdown, or a strategic shift that had not yet shown up anywhere else. He was learning to read the organization through its numbers, rather than reading the numbers in isolation.

This was not formal education. No one sat him down and explained the epistemology of financial data. It happened through exposure — through the questions he heard senior colleagues ask, through the corrections he received when his interpretation missed something important, through the accumulated texture of a thousand small moments in which he was wrong, or almost wrong, and learned from the gap. Over time, that texture became intuition. And that intuition — the ability to look at a set of numbers and sense what was actually going on behind them — is precisely what distinguished a CFO from a very good accountant.

The researchers Ikujiro Nonaka and Hirotaka Takeuchi spent years studying exactly this phenomenon — how knowledge moves through organizations, and what determines whether it takes root or evaporates. Their central finding was that tacit knowledge, the kind Polanyi described, cannot simply be documented and distributed. It has to be transferred through shared experience — through what they called "socialization": working alongside someone, observing how they approach problems, being corrected in real time, absorbing not just what decisions are made but how they are made and on what basis.[2] The junior analyst sitting near a seasoned finance director was not just learning accounting. He was, in Nonaka and Takeuchi's terms, being socialized into a way of seeing — a framework for interpretation that the senior professional had built over decades and could not have written down even if asked to.

*"The apprenticeship chain worked not because it was efficient, but because it was honest about how judgment actually forms: slowly, through friction, in context."*

This process had a name in the trades. It was called apprenticeship. You worked alongside someone who knew more than you. You watched. You imitated. You made mistakes under conditions where the mistakes were recoverable and instructive. You received feedback — not always gentle, but always grounded in reality. And over years, the master's judgment became, in some transmuted form, your own. The organizational equivalent of this was rarely as formalized, but the mechanism was identical. A generation of business leaders was produced by a system that was, at its core, an apprenticeship chain — each level of an organization transmitting hard-won judgment downward to the people who would eventually replace them.

What made this system work was not hierarchy. It was not authority, or deference, or tradition. What made it work was friction.

Friction is not a popular concept. Efficiency culture has spent decades treating it as a problem to be eliminated. But friction, in the context of human development, is not waste — it is the medium through which judgment is formed. When a junior analyst had to build a financial model by hand, reconciling line by line across multiple sources, the friction of that process was not the enemy of insight. It was the mechanism of insight. The places where the data did not add up were the places where the organization's complexity was forcing itself into view. Every discrepancy was a question: why doesn't this reconcile? And every answer to that question was a small accumulation of contextual understanding — an addition to the growing picture of how this business actually worked, as opposed to how it was supposed to work.

Friction also produced a second, subtler benefit: it created the conditions for feedback. When work was done slowly and by hand, errors were visible. When errors were visible, they could be corrected. When they were corrected — by someone more experienced, in a context where the correction could be understood rather than simply applied — the correction became part of the junior professional's developing framework for the world.

This is the mechanism that the psychologist Anders Ericsson spent a career studying. His research on expert performance across fields as varied as chess, surgery, music, and sport converged on a finding that challenges the popular notion of innate talent: expertise is not born, it is built — through what he called "deliberate practice," a specific mode of effortful engagement in which performance is stretched just beyond current capacity, errors are made, and feedback is immediate and specific.[3] The critical condition in Ericsson's model is not repetition per se — it is the quality of the feedback loop. Practice without feedback produces habit. Practice with feedback produces expertise. The difference, accumulated over thousands of hours, is what separates a competent professional from an exceptional one.

The apprenticeship chain was, in this sense, a deliberate practice engine — not by design, but by circumstance. It placed individuals in situations of genuine complexity, with real stakes, and surrounded them with more experienced colleagues whose corrections and judgments served as continuous, proximate feedback. That feedback loop, repeated across years and an expanding range of problems, is what produced judgment. Not the time. Not the hierarchy. The loop.

Here is the practical definition of judgment that matters for this book — not the philosophical one, but the organizational one. Judgment is the capacity to combine knowledge, experience, and context to reach a conclusion under conditions of uncertainty. It is, specifically, the ability to relate things: to look at a situation and recognize which of its features are relevant, which precedents apply, which dynamics are at play beneath the surface. A person exercising judgment is not following a rule — she is pattern-matching at a level of abstraction that cannot be reduced to rules. And that capacity is not innate. It is accumulated, through exactly the process described above.

What judgment looks like in practice — when it is absent — is instructive. It does not present itself as ignorance. It presents itself as a disconnect between the decision and its consequences. A senior leader cuts costs without understanding the operational texture of the team being cut: the result is not merely a cost reduction, but the destruction of a capability that took years to build and whose value was nowhere on any dashboard. A junior professional is asked to weigh in on a market entry decision without ever having been exposed to the dynamics of that market: she produces a technically competent analysis that misses the political dimensions entirely, because those dimensions were never visible to her from where she sat.

In both cases — at the top of the hierarchy and the bottom — the failure looks the same from the outside. A decision was made that should not have been made, or made differently. But the cause in both cases is structural, not personal. Neither individual lacked intelligence or effort. What they lacked was the formation that context provides — the slow, cumulative exposure to how the pieces connect, which is the only way judgment is ever actually built.

This is not a new observation. What is new is its urgency. For most of the last century, the occasional leader who rose too fast, or the analyst placed too early in too complex a situation, was an exception — a gap in an otherwise functioning system. The system compensated. The chain held. What has changed — what this book is arguing has changed fundamentally — is that the conditions which allowed the chain to hold have been systematically removed. Not in one moment, but in a sequence of entirely rational decisions, each of which made organizations more efficient and, in aggregate, made them less capable of producing the judgment they will eventually need.

The apprenticeship chain was never perfect. It was slow. It was opaque — much of what was being transmitted was transmitted implicitly, which meant that who you happened to sit near, who your first manager was, which projects you were given in your first three years, mattered enormously and unjustly. It reproduced existing power structures. It excluded people who did not fit the cultural template of the existing leadership tier. These were real costs, and they deserve acknowledgment.

But the system also produced something that we are only now beginning to understand was not incidental to it — something we assumed would persist through whatever transformations came next. It produced leaders who had, at multiple stages of their careers, been genuinely responsible for outcomes they could not fully control, in contexts they did not fully understand, with stakes that were real. That experience — of consequential uncertainty, navigated over time — is what produced the generation of leaders currently running the world's major organizations.

The question this book is asking is a simple one: who comes after them?

The apprenticeship chain that produced them has been quietly, almost invisibly, dismantled. Not by accident. Not by negligence. By logic — the same relentless logic of efficiency and scale that has driven every other transformation of organizational life over the past three decades. The same logic that brought us automation. And, now, AI.

The chain was broken one link at a time. And we did not notice, because the leaders it had already produced were still in place, still providing the judgment the system required. The vacancy is forming behind them. Slowly. Invisibly. In the space where the next generation was supposed to be formed.

That is the judgment vacuum. And understanding how it was created — what exactly was lost, and how — begins here, with what the chain was, and why it worked.

**Notes**

1. Michael Polanyi, The Tacit Dimension (Doubleday, 1966). The full formulation — "we can know more than we can tell" — appears in the opening chapter and became one of the most cited propositions in the philosophy of knowledge and organizational learning.

2. Ikujiro Nonaka and Hirotaka Takeuchi, The Knowledge-Creating Company: How Japanese Companies Create the Dynamics of Innovation (Oxford University Press, 1995). Their four-mode model of knowledge conversion — socialization, externalization, combination, internalization — remains the foundational framework in organizational knowledge management.

3. K. Anders Ericsson, Ralf Th. Krampe, and Clemens Tesch-Römer, "The Role of Deliberate Practice in the Acquisition of Expert Performance," Psychological Review 100 (1993): 363–406. Ericsson's later popular synthesis, Peak: Secrets from the New Science of Expertise (Houghton Mifflin Harcourt, 2016), co-authored with Robert Pool, extends the framework to

organizational and professional development contexts.

# 2

# The Efficiency Trap

*How automation was sold as progress, and how its hidden cost was paid in human formation.*

I spent a significant part of my career doing exactly what this chapter is about. Redesigning processes. Eliminating steps that added cost without adding value. Implementing systems that made organizations faster, more reliable, less dependent on individual heroics. I believed in it — and I was right to. The efficiency gains were real. The organizations that made those transformations became genuinely more capable, in the ways that organizations are usually measured.

It took much longer to see what the model was missing.

Not because the efficiency logic was wrong. It wasn't. But because what it was missing was not visible inside the frame it used to evaluate itself. The gains appeared on the report. The cost did not. And what doesn't appear on the report does not, in most organizations, get protected.

This chapter is about that invisible cost. Not as an argument against automation — that argument was correctly lost before most of us entered the workforce. But as an account of something that happened inside the efficiency project that we did not intend, did not measure, and are only now beginning to understand: the systematic removal of the conditions through which business judgment is formed.

## The Arithmetic That Was Hard to Argue With

The first wave of serious business automation arrived in the 1980s and 1990s wearing the language of survival. Organizations in mature markets faced a compressing logic: labor costs in developed economies were rising; technology costs were falling; the companies that made the substitution fastest would have a structural cost advantage that their competitors could not easily close. This was not ideology. It was arithmetic.

The consulting industry helped translate that arithmetic into organizational action. Re-engineering, as Michael Hammer and James Champy framed it in their 1993 manifesto, was not primarily a technology strategy — it was a process strategy: examine everything you do, eliminate what doesn't add value, and redesign what remains for maximum efficiency. The technology was the enabler. The logic was relentless.[1]

The organizations that implemented this logic well became measurably better at what they measured. Error rates fell. Cycle times compressed. Variance in outputs reduced. Costs came down. These were genuine improvements, and it would be dishonest to characterize them otherwise. The efficiency era made organizations more reliable and more scalable. It freed people from genuinely low-value work and allowed them to focus on more complex problems.

What the logic did not contain was a category for what the low-value work had also been doing. Because "adding value" was defined narrowly — outputs delivered, costs controlled — the developmental dimension of work was simply outside the frame. Formation was not a line item. It was not a deliverable. And so, when the work was redesigned or removed, the formation that had been embedded in it was removed too. Not by decision. By omission.

## When Variance Was the Curriculum

The ERP revolution deepened this dynamic in ways that were particularly consequential for junior professionals. Systems like SAP and Oracle, implemented across industries through the late 1990s and 2000s, standardized the transactional layer of organizational life. Procurement, finance, HR, supply chain — the routine operations of complex organizations were systematized into workflows that enforced consistency and reduced variance.

The organizations that implemented these systems well became genuinely more reliable. The variance in their outputs fell. The errors in their processes decreased. By every operational metric, this was progress.

But variance, it turns out, is not always a problem. In a formation context, variance is often the curriculum. The junior finance professional who spent three days chasing a reconciliation discrepancy was not wasting her time. She was learning, in the most visceral possible way, something about how her organization's processes actually worked, as opposed to how they were supposed to work. She was also learning something about herself: how to stay methodical under pressure, how to know when to escalate and when to keep digging, how to distinguish a data entry error from a structural problem in the business.

When that reconciliation was automated — when the system caught the variance and flagged it before any human being had to engage with it — the error rate went down. And so did the formation.

This is not an argument for reintroducing manual reconciliation. It is an observation about what was happening inside the work that the efficiency model did not account for. The process was redesigned for its output. Its developmental function was not in the design brief.

# The Abstraction Ladder

The efficiency era produced a generation of tools designed to abstract humans away from the operational layer. Dashboards replaced ledgers. Automated reports replaced manual consolidations. Workflow systems replaced the judgment calls that had previously been made about routing, sequencing, and prioritization. Each step up the abstraction ladder was presented as progress, and in operational terms it was. Humans operating at higher levels of abstraction could oversee more, coordinate more, decide more. Organizations became leaner.

But there is a developmental problem with abstraction, and it operates in precisely the opposite direction to the efficiency gain. To develop judgment, you need contact with the underlying reality. Not permanent contact — that would simply be inefficiency. But sufficient contact, at the right moments in a career, to build the internalized model of how the pieces fit together that is the prerequisite for effective pattern-matching later.

The psychologist Gary Klein spent decades studying how experts in high-stakes domains — firefighters, military commanders, intensive care nurses — actually make decisions under pressure. His finding, developed into what he called Recognition-Primed Decision making, was that experts do not primarily reason through options. They recognize situations. They perceive, almost instantaneously, which features of a problem are diagnostic, what category it belongs to, and what response it calls for. That recognition is not instinct — it is the crystallized residue of thousands of prior encounters with similar situations, refined through feedback.[2]

What Klein's work implies for organizational development is uncomfortable: you cannot build pattern-recognition without the patterns. The senior leader who can walk into a troubled operation and know within an hour where the real problems are is not demonstrating intelligence in the abstract. She is demonstrating the accumulated return on a career's worth of exposure to operations in various states of health and distress. She learned to recognize the dynamics of a culture under pressure because she had been in enough rooms where those dynamics were present. No dashboard would have taught her that. No abstraction could have conveyed it.

The efficiency era removed that exposure from organizational careers on a systematic basis. It was not a decision that anyone made. It was the aggregate consequence of ten thousand rational local decisions, each of which made the work faster and cleaner and more scalable — and each of which, invisibly, reduced the developmental texture of the work itself.

## The Outsourcing Amplifier

The efficiency logic did not stop at automation. It extended to the geography of work itself. Beginning in the 1990s and accelerating through the 2000s, the transactional and operational layers of organizational life migrated — to shared service centers, to outsourced providers, to offshore operations in lower-cost geographies. The same arithmetic drove the decision: if the work must be done, do it where it costs least.

The business case was often robust. The developmental case was rarely examined.

What moved offshore in most of these transitions was not just cost. It was the bottom of the organization's formation pyramid — the entry-level work through which junior professionals had previously built their operational understanding of the business. Finance transactional processing. IT help-desk. Procurement operations. HR administration. These were not glamorous functions. But they were the functions in which a young professional could learn, through daily engagement with the raw material of organizational life, what a business actually was.

The professionals who went on to lead those offshore and outsourced functions did develop — often into formidable process experts, technically skilled and operationally rigorous. But they developed expertise in a domain progressively decoupled from the business outcomes those processes were meant to serve. Process mastery deepened. The connection between that mastery and strategic understanding narrowed. A shared service center that ran an impeccable purchase-to-pay process could simultaneously employ people with no feel for why the purchasing decisions being processed were being made, what commercial logic they reflected, or what happened to the business when they were wrong.

What remained in the headquarters organization was a set of higher-level roles from which you could oversee the outputs of processes you no longer participated in. The formation logic of those roles was intact — in the sense that they involved complex problems and real stakes. But the prerequisite formation that should have preceded them, the foundational exposure that should have been building for three to five years in the junior professional's career, had been replaced by something thinner: familiarity with a system, rather than understanding of what the system was doing and why.

The result, visible in data from executive recruiters by the early 2010s, was a skills gap that was puzzling in its specificity. Organizations did not lack intelligent, well-educated young professionals. They lacked young professionals who could operate comfortably with ambiguity in complex operational environments — who could connect a process anomaly to a business implication, or read an operational problem as a signal about something deeper. The cognitive skills were present. The contextual formation that would have linked those skills to organizational reality was not.

# Efficiency Culture as a Value System

There is a deeper dimension to the efficiency trap that goes beyond any specific technology or restructuring decision. Over the decades in which automation and outsourcing remade the organizational landscape, efficiency became not merely a practice but a culture — a set of values that shaped how organizations thought about people, time, and the purpose of work itself.

In an efficiency culture, time spent doing something that does not directly produce an output is waste. Learning time, reflection time, the time it takes to do something slowly enough to understand it — none of these appear on a productivity report. They are invisible to the metrics that organizations use to evaluate themselves. And because they are invisible, they are systematically undervalued — and just as systematically cut.

This is the deepest mechanism of the efficiency trap. It is not merely that specific processes were automated. It is that the cultural frame through which organizations evaluated their own operations rendered developmental time invisible as a category. The question that efficiency culture asks — "what is the fastest, cheapest way to produce this output?" — structurally excludes the developmental question: "what are the people doing this work learning from doing it?"

When those two questions are in conflict — when the fastest way to produce the output is to automate it, but the slower way is the one that educates the person doing it — efficiency culture provides a clear and automatic answer. And that answer, reproduced across thousands of decisions over three decades, has been steadily dismantling the conditions of human formation at the base of our organizations.

Frederick Winslow Taylor, whose Principles of Scientific Management launched the efficiency movement a century ago, was explicit about the trade-off he was making. He wanted to move knowledge out of the workers' heads and into the system — to make the system, not the human, the repository of organizational intelligence.[3] In Taylor's era, this was arguably the right trade-off. The system's intelligence was bounded; the human remained essential for everything the system could not handle. What Taylor could not have anticipated is a world in which the system's intelligence grows without limit — and in which the human, stripped progressively of the operational formation that once happened as a matter of course, finds herself with less and less to contribute when the system reaches its edge.

## What Was Lost, Precisely

It is worth being precise about what the efficiency era removed, because the claim is sometimes misunderstood. This is not a nostalgic argument for doing things the hard way. Automation genuinely made organizations more reliable, more scalable, and less dependent on the heroic judgment of individuals operating in chaotic processes. Those were real gains, and they matter.

What was lost was something more specific, and it is important to locate it correctly. The people who designed and implemented automation — who mapped the processes, identified the logic, built the systems — often emerged from that work with a deeper understanding of the business than almost anyone else in it. To automate something well, you have to understand it thoroughly. The act of making a process explicit, of encoding its logic into a system, is itself a powerful form of formation.

The formation loss is not theirs. It belongs to the generation that came after.

The philosopher Albert Borgmann described this as the difference between a "device" and a "focal practice." A device conceals its workings and delivers a commodity. A focal practice engages the whole person — requires skill, attention, effort — and in doing so develops the person who engages in it.[4] The professional who inherits an automated system inherits a device. She can operate it. She can optimize it at the margins. What she does not inherit is the understanding that produced its design — the encoded judgment of the person who had to think through every edge case, every exception, every point of failure, in order to make the thing work.

That understanding is not documented anywhere, because it does not need to be — it is in the system. Until the system needs to change, or fails in an unfamiliar way, or needs to be evaluated against a new strategic context. At that point, the organization discovers that what it has is operators and what it needed were understanders. That gap — between being able to run something and being able to reason about it — is where the formation loss ultimately surfaces.

# The Organization That Forgot How It Worked

There is a phenomenon that became visible in the 2010s across industries where automation had been most thorough: the organization that could no longer fully explain itself. Processes that had been automated years earlier continued to function — until they didn't. When they failed, or needed to be changed, or needed to be evaluated against a new strategic reality, organizations discovered that the people who understood why those processes had been designed the way they were had moved on. Their successors had operated the systems. They had not inherited the reasoning behind them.

This plays out in recognizable ways. A pricing model that the commercial team has used for years, that everyone knows how to run, that nobody fully understands how to challenge — because the assumptions built into it were encoded by someone who has long since left. A supply chain configuration that was optimized for a cost structure that no longer exists, but that resists redesign because the people running it have never had to design anything. An ERP implementation whose logic, by the time it needs to be replaced, can be reverse-engineered from the system but cannot be recovered from the people — because those people never had to hold it in their heads.

In each case, the organization functions normally — until it needs to exercise the kind of judgment that only deep operational formation can provide. And at that point it discovers that the pipeline of people who could provide it is thinner than anyone had noticed.

These are not failure stories in the dramatic sense. They are ordinary organizational life, in organizations that were run well by every available metric. The efficiency gains were real. The reliability improvements were genuine. The cost reductions were delivered. What was not measured — and therefore what was not managed — was the gradual thinning of operational understanding at every level as the formation that used to happen organically inside the work was, piece by piece, engineered out of it.

## The Argument That Wasn't Made

The most important thing about the efficiency trap is that the developmental cost was never part of the argument. Not because the people making the automation decisions were careless or negligent. I was one of those people, and I was neither. But because the cost was not visible in the frame we were using.

Organizations know how to measure process efficiency. They have decades of tools, methodologies, and metrics for it. They do not know how to measure the developmental value of the work they are automating away. There is no line item for "contextual formation accrued." There is no metric for "judgment pipeline depth." The efficiency gain appears on the report. The formation loss does not.

This is the heart of the trap. It is not a failure of intention. It is a failure of measurement — a systematic blind spot built into the evaluative framework that organizations use to make decisions about their own operations. And in the absence of measurement, what is invisible is also what is unprotected.

The automation decisions of the last thirty years were, in isolation, almost always defensible. Each one traded a real cost for a real gain. The problem was that the costs and gains being compared were not the full set of costs and gains. The developmental dimension was not in the room. Not because we wanted to exclude it. Because we did not have a way to see it.

Now it needs to be seen. Because what was lost through automation — the organic formation of contextual understanding through operational proximity and friction — cannot be recovered by doing less automation. The clock does not run backward. The economics do not reverse. What can be done is what this book will eventually argue for: the deliberate, intentional re-creation of the conditions that produce judgment, inside the new organizational reality rather than as a nostalgic retreat from it.

But that argument requires, first, a complete account of what was lost. And the efficiency era, significant as it was, is not the final act. It was the preparation for something more consequential — the arrival of a technology that does not merely automate the task, but automates the reasoning behind the task. The implications of that arrival are the subject of the next chapter.

**Notes**

1. Michael Hammer and James Champy, Reengineering the Corporation: A Manifesto for Business Revolution (HarperBusiness, 1993). The book sold over three million copies and launched one of the most influential — and most controversial — management movements of the late twentieth century. Critics later noted that the "re-engineering" label was applied to many initiatives that were primarily cost-reduction exercises with limited process redesign.

2. Gary Klein, Sources of Power: How People Make Decisions (MIT Press, 1998). Klein's Recognition-Primed Decision model emerged from field

research with firefighters and military commanders, and has since been applied extensively in organizational and leadership development contexts.

3. Frederick Winslow Taylor, The Principles of Scientific Management (Harper & Brothers, 1911). Taylor's explicit goal was to transfer knowledge from workers to management — to make the system, not the individual, the repository of organizational intelligence.

4. Albert Borgmann, Technology and the Character of Contemporary Life: A Philosophical Inquiry (University of Chicago Press, 1984). Borgmann's distinction between devices and focal practices provides a philosophical framework for understanding what is at stake in the progressive automation of human work — not merely the loss of jobs, but the loss of the formative engagement that meaningful work provides.

# 3

# The AI Accelerant

*Why AI doesn't just continue the trend — it breaks the remaining feedback loops entirely and compresses the timeline to crisis.*

There is a useful way to think about what the previous two chapters have been describing. The efficiency era delivered real and lasting gains. Organizations became more reliable, more scalable, and less dependent on individual heroics. The unintended consequence — invisible inside the evaluative frames organizations used to measure themselves — was something else entirely: the quiet removal of the conditions through which the next generation would have built its judgment. The entry-level work that had served as the organizational curriculum was automated, standardized, or relocated. The friction through which judgment had always formed was engineered out of the system. Not by decision. By omission.

But there is something important to note about that era, something that matters for understanding what comes next. The efficiency wave moved vertically, and it moved slowly. One process at a time. One function at a time. One layer of the organization at a time. The disruption was serious, but it was sequential — which meant organizations had something they rarely had time to appreciate until it was gone: room to adapt. New roles emerged. Professionals who could no longer build their formation through manual reconciliation could instead develop it through process redesign, systems implementation, data management. The pipeline thinned. But the organization had time to absorb the change, to develop workarounds, to maintain at least some of the feedback loops that judgment requires.

Artificial intelligence does not move vertically. It does not take one process at a time. It is, in the precise sense of the word, horizontal — reaching simultaneously across every domain of expertise, every function, every level of organizational life, at a speed that renders incremental adaptation impossible. The question is not whether this is a continuation of the efficiency trend. It is whether it is something categorically different.

# Not a Tool. A Mirror.

The temptation, when thinking about AI in organizations, is to reach for the familiar analogy: AI is a more powerful version of the tools that came before. The spreadsheet replaced the ledger. The ERP system replaced the spreadsheet. AI replaces the ERP system. Each step in this sequence automated more of the work, freed up more human time for higher-order tasks, and accelerated the efficiency gains that organizations had been pursuing for decades. On this reading, AI is simply the next wave — faster, broader, more powerful, but structurally continuous with what preceded it.

This reading is wrong, and it is wrong in a way that matters enormously for what follows.

What made previous automation waves categorically different from AI is precisely this: they automated execution. They took tasks that humans had previously performed — calculation, data entry, workflow routing, transaction processing — and moved those tasks into systems. The human remained responsible for the reasoning behind the task: the interpretation, the judgment about what the output meant, the contextual understanding that connected the process to the business outcome it was supposed to serve.

The system executed. The human understood — or was at least supposed to.

Generative AI does something different. It does not merely automate the execution of a task. It engages with the reasoning layer — the part of the work that, in every previous wave of automation, remained human. It reads the context, interprets the data, synthesizes across sources, constructs the argument, drafts the recommendation. It does the thing that used to require a human to think.

And here is where precision becomes essential, because a common mis-reading of this argument is that AI's reasoning is somehow inferior — a simulacrum that looks like thought but lacks the genuine article. That is not the argument. The argument is almost the opposite, and it is more unsettling.

## The Superiority Problem

Consider what a human professional actually brings to a cognitive task. A finance professional, to use a concrete example, has built a knowledge base over years of study and experience. He understands accounting rules, financial modeling, the dynamics of markets, the logic of capital allocation. That knowledge is deep, within its domain, and hard-won. It represents a genuine expertise.

But it is also bounded. His processing capacity has real limits. He can hold a certain volume of data in mind at once. His knowledge is domain-constrained — deep in some areas, inevitably thin in others. He builds it linearly, one year of experience at a time, one domain at a time. The accumulation is sequential, slow, and narrow relative to the scope of the problems he will eventually be asked to address.

A large language model brings something categorically different to the same task. It has been trained on a corpus of human-generated text spanning hundreds of domains — science, finance, law, history, strategy, organizational behavior, and the vast surrounding territory of human intellectual production — orders of magnitude broader than any individual could accumulate in a career. Its processing speed is not the speed of a careful analyst working through a model — it is the speed of a machine that can synthesize across that entire corpus in seconds, returning output that would take any individual human a significant multiple of the available time to produce.

This is not a technology that is marginally better than the human it assists. In the specific dimensions of breadth, speed, and volume of reference, it is not in the same category. The gap is not one of degree. It is one of kind.

And this is precisely why AI represents something more dangerous to human formation than anything that came before it — not because it is inferior, but because it is genuinely, demonstrably superior at many of the cognitive tasks that used to constitute the training ground for professional judgment. When the AI's answer is better than the answer the human would have produced alone, the human has no experiential reason to do the work themselves. The rational signal is clear: delegate to the system.

The efficiency era produced a similar signal, and we have spent two chapters tracing its consequences. But the efficiency signal applied to execution — to tasks that were routine, definable, codable. The AI signal applies to reasoning — to the cognitive engagement that, precisely because it was effortful and imperfect and slow, produced the internalized models that judgment is built from.

When AI provides the reasoning directly, the professional gets the output without the formation. And because the output is excellent — often superior to what he would have produced himself — there is no visible signal that anything has been lost.

# What Is Actually Lost

It is worth being precise about this, because the formation loss in the AI era is more subtle than in the efficiency era, and therefore more difficult to see and defend against.

In the efficiency era, what was lost was contact with the material. The junior finance professional who no longer had to build the consolidation by hand lost the feel for which numbers were stable and which were constructed, which relationships in the data were causal and which were incidental.

In the AI era, the material is still present. The professional is still engaging with the problem. She is reading the AI's output, evaluating it, asking follow-up questions, directing the analysis. She appears to be thinking. The appearance is not entirely false — something cognitive is happening. But the specific cognitive act that would have built her judgment is not happening. She is not constructing the model. She is not navigating the ambiguity. She is not discovering, through the discomfort of being wrong, where her understanding has gaps.

She is, instead, directing a system that thinks for her. And the difference between directing a system that thinks and thinking yourself is precisely the difference between operating a device and developing a capacity.

There is a well-documented analogy at a smaller scale that illuminates the mechanism. Research on GPS navigation and spatial memory has found that habitual GPS use is associated with a measurable decline in hippocampus-dependent spatial memory — the internal cognitive mapping that allows people to navigate without external guidance.[1] The finding is not that GPS users navigate less well. They navigate just as well, or better, precisely because the GPS is doing the work. The finding is that when the GPS is removed — when the person is required to navigate from their own internal resources — their capacity to do so has atrophied in proportion to how much they had delegated to the device.

The mechanism is instructive: the person did not become less intelligent. They became less practiced in a specific cognitive act. And the practice of that act — the effortful construction of a mental map through attention and engagement with the environment — was precisely what developed and maintained the underlying capacity.

The professional who delegates the reasoning layer to AI is navigating with GPS. They arrive at the destination reliably. They do not build the map.

## The Feedback Loop That Is No Longer Closing

The formation argument in this book has always been, at its core, an argument about feedback loops. Judgment is built not through exposure alone but through a specific cycle: attempt, error, feedback, revision, internalization. The apprenticeship chain worked because it embedded professionals in conditions where that cycle could repeat, across thousands of instances, across years. Ericsson's deliberate practice research was precise about this: expertise requires not merely repetition, but repetition with immediate, specific feedback that allows errors to be corrected and performance to be stretched.[2] The feedback loop is not an optional feature of professional formation. It is the mechanism.

The efficiency era weakened this loop by reducing the volume and variety of the situations in which junior professionals were required to attempt things, make errors, and receive corrections. The loop ran more slowly, because the raw material of formation — the problems that required genuine engagement — had been automated away from the entry level.

AI breaks the loop in a different and more fundamental way. It does not merely reduce the frequency of the cycle. It intercepts the cycle at its most critical point: the attempt itself. If the attempt is delegated — if the professional asks the AI to produce the analysis rather than constructing it themselves — then there is no error, and therefore no feedback, and therefore no revision, and therefore no internalization. The loop does not run slowly. It does not run.

What replaces it is something that looks like a feedback loop but is not one. The professional evaluates the AI's output. He may approve it, or query it, or ask for revisions. He is exercising a kind of judgment — the judgment of evaluation rather than construction. But evaluative judgment and constructive judgment are not the same capability, and they do not develop each other. The person who can tell a good argument from a poor one has not necessarily acquired the capacity to construct a good argument under conditions of uncertainty.

This distinction — between evaluative competence and constructive competence — is where the formation loss in the AI era is most precisely located. And it is a distinction that is very difficult to see from the outside, because both look like professional engagement with an analytical problem.

There is a second-order consequence that compounds this further. The quality of what AI produces is not independent of the human directing it. It is directly shaped by the quality of the prompt — by the precision of the question asked, the specificity of the context provided, the depth of understanding the human brings to framing what she needs. A formed professional, with genuine domain knowledge and contextual judgment, asks different questions than one whose formation is thin. She knows what she doesn't know. She can name the ambiguity she needs resolved. She can push back on an output that is technically correct but strategically wrong, because she has the underlying model to recognize the difference.

What this means is that the formation loss is not merely a problem that runs parallel to AI adoption. It degrades the human-AI partnership itself over time. Shallower formation produces shallower prompts. Shallower prompts produce less useful outputs. The gap between what AI could contribute to a well-directed partnership and what it actually contributes to a poorly-directed one is not fixed — it widens as the human capacity to direct it well declines. This is not a technology problem. It is a formation problem that expresses itself as a technology problem.

## The Horizontal Sweep

The efficiency era's formation loss was serious but bounded, because it operated on specific functions, at specific levels, over specific time horizons. A CFO who had built her judgment through years of hands-on engagement with operational finance was not directly affected by the automation of transactional processing. She already had the formation. The loss fell on the generation coming after her — those who inherited the automated systems without inheriting the understanding that had produced their design.

AI's reach is not bounded in this way. It is, as noted, horizontal — touching every domain simultaneously, at every level of the organization. It reaches not just the entry-level analyst but the mid-career manager constructing the strategic options paper. Not just the junior associate but the senior partner reviewing the client recommendation. The formation loss does not fall only on one generation, at one level, in one function. It distributes across the entire organization at once.

This is what makes the speed of AI adoption so consequential. The efficiency era played out over three decades, which was slow enough that the leaders who had formed in the pre-automation environment were still in place when the consequences of the formation loss began to emerge. They provided, through their own embodied judgment, the organizational guidance that the depleted pipeline could not. They were, in a sense, the reserve — the living repository of accumulated contextual understanding that allowed organizations to navigate complexity even after the conditions that had produced it had been dismantled.

That reserve is not unlimited. The generation that formed before automation is in the final decade of its organizational tenure. The next generation formed in a partially automated environment — the efficiency era's inheritance — and is now the primary leadership tier. Behind them, a generation that has formed in an AI-enabled environment is entering the ranks of mid-level management. The progression compresses. The pipeline is not merely thin. It is thinning faster, at every level, than the formation conditions of any era have been able to replenish it.

Organizational judgment is not unlike a natural resource — one that is renewable, but only under specific conditions and only at a specific rate. The efficiency era accelerated consumption of that resource beyond the natural rate of replenishment. The resource did not run out, because the accumulated stock from previous generations was still in the system. AI accelerates the consumption further, while simultaneously degrading the conditions under which the resource renews itself. We are approaching the point where the stock that sustained us is no longer adequate to the demand placed on it — and the conditions for renewal have not been deliberately recreated.

## The Seduction of the Visible

There is one further dimension to the AI accelerant that distinguishes it from every previous wave of automation, and it deserves to be named directly because it is the most difficult to argue against in organizational settings.

AI's output is not merely useful. It is impressive. It is articulate, contextually sensitive, apparently reasoned, and often genuinely insightful. It does not look like automation. It looks like intelligence. And that appearance does something to the humans who encounter it that no previous technology has done — it creates a distorted mirror of capability.

The professional who uses AI to produce a sophisticated strategic analysis has not merely been given a tool that makes her more efficient. She has been given something that makes her appear to herself — and to those around her — more capable than her underlying formation would independently support. The output is excellent. The formation that produced it is the AI's, not hers. But the two are not easily distinguishable from the outside. And they are not always distinguishable from the inside.

This is the impostor mechanism, and it deserves serious attention. The feedback loop that normally calibrates a professional's self-knowledge — I attempted this, I fell short in this specific way, I understand where my edge is — is bypassed. What replaces it is not a more accurate self-model. It is a flattered one. The professional produces excellent outputs and has no reliable map of what she actually understands, where her judgment genuinely functions, and where she would fail if the system were unavailable.

The efficiency era at least had the virtue of making formation loss visible when the system failed. When the process broke down, or needed to be redesigned, or needed to be evaluated against a new strategic context, organizations discovered that the people who understood the underlying logic had moved on. The failure was detectable, even if it was expensive.

AI's formation loss may be less detectable, because the system rarely fails in obvious ways. It produces confident, articulate outputs in almost every situation. The professional who has navigated with AI for a decade does not discover the gap in his formation when the GPS loses signal — because the GPS rarely loses signal. He discovers it, if he discovers it at all, only in the situations that require the deepest and most irreducible forms of human judgment: the stakeholder conflict that cannot be resolved by analysis, the organizational crisis that requires someone who has been through enough crises to know how they feel, the strategic decision whose most important dimensions are not in any data set.

These are, of course, the most consequential situations that organizations face. And they are precisely the situations that AI cannot, in its current form, resolve.

## The One Thing That Cannot Be Processed

It is important to be clear about why, because the argument is sometimes made too clumsily — as though AI simply lacks something, as though it is missing a module that will eventually be developed and installed. The deficit is not of that kind.

AI processes data. All the data it has ever ingested has been data about human experience — what people have observed, recorded, described, and analyzed. But experience and the record of experience are not the same thing. What the record cannot contain is the felt quality of judgment under genuine uncertainty: the discomfort of not knowing, the weight of consequence, the reading of a room, the recognition of what is unsaid in a conversation, the embodied sense of whether an organization is healthy or sick that comes from having been in enough organizations to have developed an internal reference for what health feels like.

These are not romantic descriptions of ineffable human qualities. They are descriptions of competencies that develop through specific kinds of experience, and that have specific organizational functions — functions that become critical precisely when the situation does not conform to pattern, when the data is insufficient, when the decision cannot wait for better information, when the human dimension of the problem is the primary dimension.

The economist Daron Acemoglu has articulated the structural version of this argument: the risk with AI is not that it becomes too good at what it does, but that it is being deployed primarily in ways that substitute for human judgment rather than augmenting it — a trajectory he describes as taking us in the wrong direction.[3] What Acemoglu frames as an economic and structural concern has a direct organizational parallel: organizations that use AI to substitute for the development of human judgment are not merely making a strategic error. They are systematically undermining the conditions under which the irreducibly human capacities — judgment, relational sensitivity, contextual wisdom — are formed and maintained.

Erik Brynjolfsson, approaching the same territory from a different direction, has identified what he calls the Turing Trap: the tendency of AI development and deployment to focus on mimicking human intelligence rather than augmenting it — on replacing human cognitive labor rather than extending human capability into domains that neither humans nor machines could previously reach.[4] The trap is not technological. It is economic and cultural: there are immediate, measurable incentives to automate, and diffuse, difficult-to-measure costs to the formation that automation displaces.

## A Different Relationship Is Possible

None of this implies that AI should be used less, or that the right response to the formation problem is a retreat from the technology. That argument was correctly lost before it could be made. The capabilities that AI brings — the breadth, the speed, the processing power, the synthesis across domains that no individual human could replicate — are real, and the organizations that fail to deploy them will simply be less capable than the ones that do.

The argument is more precise, and more demanding. It concerns not whether AI is used, but how — specifically, whether it is deployed in ways that substitute for human formation or in ways that work alongside it. There is a version of AI adoption in which the technology amplifies what formed humans can do — in which the AI's breadth and processing power are directed by human judgment that has been deliberately cultivated and tested. And there is a version in which the technology substitutes for the formation of human judgment — in which the speed and quality of AI output creates a set of incentives that systematically bypass the conditions under which judgment develops.

The first version requires something the second does not: a deliberate, organizational commitment to maintaining the conditions of human formation alongside the deployment of AI capability. Not as a sentimental gesture toward human dignity. But as a clear-eyed organizational decision about what the organization needs its humans to be able to do — not just today, when the AI is available and functioning well, but in the situations that reveal what humans alone can provide.

The efficiency era broke the chain, link by link, over thirty years. AI has not broken a link. It has changed the nature of the chain itself. And the organizations that do not understand that distinction — that treat AI as a faster version of what came before, rather than as a different kind of challenge to a different kind of human capacity — will be the ones that discover the vacuum not in retrospect, but in crisis.

**Notes**

1. Louisa Dahmani and Véronique D. Bohbot, "Habitual use of GPS negatively impacts spatial memory during self-guided navigation," Scientific Reports 10 (2020): 6310. The study found that greater lifetime GPS experience was associated with worse spatial memory during self-guided navigation, with longitudinal data suggesting the decline deepens with continued use.

2. K. Anders Ericsson, Ralf Th. Krampe, and Clemens Tesch-Römer, "The Role of Deliberate Practice in the Acquisition of Expert Performance," Psychological Review 100 (1993): 363–406.

3. Daron Acemoglu, "Rebalancing AI," Finance & Development (International Monetary Fund, December 2023). Acemoglu's concern is that current AI deployment is directed primarily at automation — substituting for human labor — rather than at augmentation, which would complement human capabilities. See also Daron Acemoglu and Simon Johnson, Power and

Progress: Our Thousand-Year Struggle Over Technology and Prosperity (PublicAffairs, 2023).

4. Erik Brynjolfsson, "The Turing Trap: The Promise & Peril of Human-Like Artificial Intelligence," Daedalus 151, no. 2 (Spring 2022): 272–287.

# 4

# The Generation Gap Nobody Talks About



*Moment II — The Vacuum*

*The current leadership tier was forged pre-automation. Behind them, the pipeline is hollow — not because of talent, but because of conditions.*

There is a conversation that happens in the margins of almost every serious succession discussion, in the gap between what is written in the slide deck and what is said quietly on the way out of the room. It sounds something like this: we have talented people — capable, well-educated, technically adept — but we are not sure they are ready. Not in the way the generation before them was ready. Something is different.

Nobody quite finishes the sentence. The concern is gestured at, then set aside, because it is not the kind of observation that fits neatly into a leadership development framework or a succession planning template. It is not a skills gap that can be closed with a training program. It is something more structural — and therefore more uncomfortable — than that.

This chapter is about that unfinished sentence. It is about why the concern is real, why it is growing, and why the silence around it is itself part of the problem.

# The Formation That Shaped a Generation

Every generation of leaders was produced by a set of conditions — not a curriculum, not a program, but a set of conditions. The conditions shaped what they encountered at each stage of their careers: what kind of complexity they were exposed to, what kind of feedback they received, what kind of consequential uncertainty they had to navigate before they were senior enough to have the institutional support to make it comfortable.

The generation currently running the world's major organizations was shaped by conditions that no longer exist. This is not a romanticization of the past — the conditions were not uniformly good, and the formation they produced was neither equitable nor fully intentional. But it was real, and what it produced was real.

Spend any time with senior leaders who built their careers in the 1990s and 2000s, and a pattern emerges that is almost universal. When they describe what actually formed them as professionals, they do not describe the skills they were trained in or the qualifications they acquired. They describe experiences of doing things by hand. Processing orders manually. Building models in physical ledgers. Managing data through systems that were slow and unforgiving enough that you were forced to understand what you were doing, rather than simply executing within a pre-designed workflow. They describe the experience of being wrong in front of people who knew more, and having to recover. Of being given responsibility before they were ready, and finding out through the discomfort of that readiness gap what they were actually made of.

There is a nostalgic quality to these descriptions — and it would be a mistake to take the nostalgia at face value. The systems those leaders worked within were not better than the systems that replaced them. They were slower, more error-prone, more dependent on individual heroics, less scalable. The efficiency gains that followed were real and, in most cases, genuinely valuable.

The question is not whether the old systems were superior. The question is what, in addition to their inefficiency, they were doing.

What they were doing — what no one designed them to do, but what they did regardless — was forming judgment. They were placing people in contact with the underlying reality of organizational life: the raw material of decisions, the friction of complexity, the feedback of consequence. Not because anyone planned it that way. Because the conditions required it.

## Two Kinds of Expertise, One Missing Bridge

The generation gap that nobody talks about is not, at its core, a gap in capability. The professionals who sit below today's senior leadership tier are, by most conventional measures, more capable than their predecessors. They have higher levels of formal education. They are more fluent with data, more adept with technology, more analytical in their approach to problems. They are, in many respects, exactly the kind of professionals that the efficiency era designed them to be.

The gap is in a different dimension: not what they can do, but what they have been through. And the specific thing they have not been through is the formation that produces the capacity to translate technical competence into organizational judgment — to connect what the data says to what it means, to understand not just the logic of a decision but the terrain of consequences in which it will land.

A concrete pattern illustrates this with unusual clarity. In the offshore delivery centers that became central to the efficiency model — the shared service operations, the analytics hubs, the process centers of excellence built across cost-effective geographies — the professionals who staffed them became, over time, genuinely formidable technical experts. Finance professionals who could construct models of remarkable sophistication. Data engineers who could manage and manipulate vast datasets with precision.

Process specialists who understood the operational logic of their systems at a level of depth that no onshore generalist could match.

But when asked about the implications of their outputs — what the numbers they had produced meant for the strategic decisions they were meant to inform — the answer was often thin. Not because the individuals were incapable of inference, but because inference of that kind requires a context that the conditions of their work had not provided. They had been formed for accuracy. They had not been formed for interpretation. The two things are not the same.

The inverse was equally revealing. Onshore professionals — the ones nominally positioned to provide the contextual interpretation — had progressively lost touch with the operational reality their teams were processing. When asked how they would redesign the reports their offshore teams produced, or how they would improve the processes those teams managed, the answer was equally thin: that, they said, was what the offshore teams were for. The bridge between the two kinds of expertise was not being built. And as the people who had once held both capabilities simultaneously — the generation who had done the analysis before the analysis was outsourced — moved toward retirement, the gap widened.

*"The concern is gestured at, then set aside, because it is not the kind of observation that fits neatly into a leadership development framework or a succession planning template."*

## What Is Actually Missing

If you press senior leaders to be specific about what they observe in the tier below them — not what they assume in the abstract, but what they actually encounter in rooms, in decisions, in high-stakes moments — the answers are more precise than the usual language of "leadership readiness" suggests.

The first thing they describe is a limited tolerance for unresolved ambiguity. The professionals they are looking to as successors are technically excellent at solving defined problems. They are less comfortable being handed a problem that has no clean edges, no established methodology, no system to run it through. The instinct, in the face of such a problem, is to frame it so that it becomes solvable by the tools available — rather than to stay with the ambiguity long enough to understand what the problem actually is. That capacity — to hold a question open, to resist the premature closure of a messy situation — is not innate. It is accumulated through repeated exposure to situations where premature closure led to visible failure.

The second is what might be called directional confidence. Many of the technically excellent professionals below the senior tier are, in practice, more comfortable following a defined direction than proposing one. They are skilled at execution, rigorous in delivery, responsive to the parameters they are given. They are less practiced at the antecedent act: standing in front of a problem with no parameters given and deciding where to begin. The capacity to initiate — to take the first step without being told which step to take — is built through experience of having to do it, repeatedly, in conditions where the stakes were real.

The third is the language of seniority. There is, in organizations that function well, a specific register that emerges at the leadership level — a way of communicating that is simultaneously precise and calibrated, that carries the weight of institutional context, that knows when to signal certainty and when to signal openness. This register is not taught. It is absorbed, through years of proximity to the level above: watching how senior leaders frame problems, observing what they choose to say and what they choose not to say, learning the political and relational texture of how consequential communication actually works. Without that proximity — without the sustained exposure to the level above that the traditional organizational pyramid provided — the register does not develop.

What is absent, in other words, is not intelligence or education or effort. It is what the organizational theorist Elliott Jaques spent decades describing as "time-span capacity": the ability to operate effectively across longer time horizons, to hold more variables in mind simultaneously, to sustain judgment across the arc of a decision that takes months or years to play out rather than days.[1] Jaques argued that this capacity was not primarily a function of innate ability — it was a function of developmental opportunity: the progressive exposure to problems of increasing complexity and increasing time horizon that the traditional organizational hierarchy, whatever its other failings, reliably provided.

## The Silence and Its Logic

The generation gap is not invisible because it is subtle. It is invisible because the incentive structure of organizational life makes it extremely uncomfortable to name.

Consider what it would mean, in practice, for an organization to state directly: the leadership tier we have built behind our current executives does not have the judgment that our current executives have, and we do not know how to produce that judgment on the timeline we need it. The statement would immediately raise questions about the effectiveness of the organization's leadership development investment — questions that would implicate the HR function, the development programs, the performance management systems, the succession planning process. It would raise questions about the current leaders themselves, whose responsibility it is to develop the people below them.

There is a measurement dimension to this silence that is equally significant. Organizations are very good at measuring what they have invested in developing their people. They are considerably worse at measuring whether the formation those investments produced is the right kind of formation. Leadership development programs are assessed on satisfaction scores, on competency ratings, on 360-degree feedback, on engagement metrics. They are not assessed on the question that actually matters: does the person who completed this program have better judgment than the person who did not?

What happened instead, across the efficiency era, was a subtle but consequential re-framing. Organizations observed that their people were becoming more technically sophisticated — more analytically capable, more data-literate, more fluent with the tools that the efficiency revolution had introduced. They measured that sophistication, found it impressive, and concluded that the pipeline was in good shape. The measurement was accurate. The inference was not. Technical sophistication and organizational judgment are not the same thing. They were once co-developed, in the conditions of the old apprenticeship chain. In the new conditions, they were being developed separately — and only one of them was being measured.

There is a further structural reason for the silence that is uncomfortable but necessary to name. The professionals who were most heavily affected by the conditions that produced this gap — those at the mid-level of organizations who migrated, by rational professional instinct, from being functional experts to being technical experts — are now caught in an increasingly difficult position. The ability to manage data systems and build analytical capability on top of legacy infrastructure was, a decade ago, a genuinely differentiating professional skill. Today, those same skills are being rapidly replicated at far greater scale and speed by AI systems. They are neither deep enough in their functional domain to provide the contextual interpretation that their organizations need, nor advanced enough in their technical domain to compete with what AI can deliver. This is not their failure. It is the product of a system that kept moving the ground beneath them.

# The Human Cost of Compression

There is a dimension of this argument that rarely appears in discussions of organizational capability, yet is inseparable from it: the physical and psychological toll of asking people to adapt faster than human beings are able to adapt.

Organizational change has always imposed adaptation costs on individuals. The efficiency transformations described in the previous chapters were disruptive, and the disruption was felt by real people. But the efficiency era, for all its pace, moved in a recognizable direction: it had a logic, and the logic could eventually be learned. A professional who understood the logic of the ERP implementation or the shared service transition could eventually adapt to it, and over a cycle of a few years, arrive at a new stable position.

The AI era does not offer that stability. The pace of change is not linear — it is exponential, and the time available for adaptation is compressing at the same rate as the changes themselves are accelerating. The consequence is beginning to appear in the data with striking clarity. Workplace burnout reached its highest recorded levels in 2024, with more than half of all employees reporting some experience of it — a 15 percentage-point increase in a single year.[2] The generational pattern within that data is particularly significant: Millennials, who represent the mid-career professionals most directly caught in the transition described in this chapter, reported burnout at 66 per cent — far higher than Gen X at 55 per cent or Baby Boomers at 39 per cent.[3] And it is the middle management layer — the very tier that sits between the retiring leadership and the AI-exposed junior levels — that reports the highest burnout rates of any organizational group.[4]

The World Health Organization formally recognized burnout as an occupational phenomenon in 2019, characterizing it as the result of chronic workplace stress that has not been successfully managed.[5] The definition points directly at what is happening here. It is not that the individuals are failing to manage their stress. It is that the system is generating stress at a rate that cannot be managed, because the rate of change has outpaced the human adaptive bandwidth that organizations implicitly depend upon.

This matters for the generation gap argument in a specific way. Burnout is not only a welfare problem — it is a formation problem. The cognitive state associated with chronic burnout is precisely the state that makes judgment formation impossible: the emotional exhaustion that precludes sustained engagement with complex problems, the cynicism that forecloses the curiosity that learning requires, the reduced efficacy that makes the experience of consequential uncertainty feel threatening rather than developmental.

## The Pyramid Becomes a Pillar

The structural evidence for the generation gap is beginning to emerge most clearly in the professional services industries that touched virtually every sector as their clients — and that were therefore among the first to feel the full effect of both the efficiency logic and the AI disruption.

The legal profession offers a particularly instructive case — not because the headline employment numbers are alarming, but because of what is happening inside the structure of legal organizations. The traditional law firm operated on a clear pyramid: armies of junior associates doing the foundational work — document review, legal research, due diligence, basic drafting — under the supervision of more senior lawyers who corrected, calibrated, and transmitted judgment in the process. That foundational work was formative. The junior associate who spent two years in document review was building, through that slow and effortful engagement with the raw material of legal complexity, the pattern recognition that would eventually make them a capable practitioner.

AI is now doing that work. Between 2005 and 2024, associates shrank as a proportion of the total fee-earning population at major US law firms, from

44.5 per cent to 40.2 per cent. Non-equity partners grew from 24 per cent to 32 per cent.[6] The pyramid is becoming a pillar. And the junior layer that is being thinned is precisely the layer through which judgment has always been formed.

The head of the National Association for Law Placement described the situation with unusual directness: firms would expect future first-year associates to start performing at the level of today's fourth-year associates, but on a much shorter runway to learn.[7] That observation contains the entire problem in compressed form. The runway to learn is the formation. Compress the runway, and you compress the formation.

The consulting industry presents the same dynamic at larger scale. The major consulting firms are now confronting a structural crisis directly related to this dynamic. McKinsey shed roughly 10 per cent of its global workforce between 2024 and early 2026. PwC, KPMG, Deloitte, Bain, and Accenture made comparable reductions.[8] Job postings for non-senior consulting roles in some markets fell 40 per cent between 2022 and 2025. The cause is not merely that AI can do some of what junior consultants do — though that is true. The deeper cause is that the consulting model was predicated on selling hours, and what clients are realizing, with AI in hand, is that what they actually needed was judgment. They were buying formation masquerading as output.

## The Retirement Clock

There is a demographic dimension to this argument that adds a specific kind of urgency. The current leadership tier is retiring. In 2024 alone, roughly 11,000 Baby Boomers reached retirement age every single day in the United States.[9] CEO departures across US companies reached 646 in the first quarter of 2025 alone — a 43 per cent increase from the same period the previous year.[10] The response, in many cases, has been to reach backward: 22 companies in the S&P 1500 reappointed former CEOs in 2024 and early

2025, making the boomerang CEO more common than at any point in the past decade.[11] That pattern is not a sign of organizational confidence. It is a sign of organizational scarcity — a board discovering, at the moment of transition, that the internal pipeline does not contain what it was supposed to contain.

What makes this more than an ordinary succession challenge is a second dynamic running in the opposite direction, and at a different pace. The capabilities of AI are not improving linearly. They are improving exponentially. Each generation of tools makes the previous generation look primitive, and the compounding effect is that the distance between what AI can do and what junior professionals are being trained to do is widening at precisely the moment when the senior professionals who bridged that distance are departing.

The intersection of these two curves — one describing the exit of judgment from organizations, the other describing the rate at which AI is absorbing the work through which judgment was historically built — is where the generation gap becomes a structural risk. Neither curve, taken alone, is catastrophic. Retirements are manageable when the pipeline is full. AI disruption is manageable when the people navigating it have the judgment to know what to do with it. The problem is the conjunction: both things happening at once, on accelerating timescales, in organizations whose measurement systems were designed to detect neither.

## The Counterargument, Taken Seriously

The pushback to this argument is predictable, and it deserves a serious response.

The first objection is historical: every generation has worried about the one behind it. This objection is partly right and partly beside the point. It is right that the concern is perennial. It is beside the point in its implied conclusion

— that because the concern has been expressed before without catastrophic consequence, it can be safely discounted now. The previous expressions of the concern were operating against a background in which the apprenticeship chain, whatever its local imperfections, was still fundamentally intact. What this book is arguing is that that mechanism has been systematically disrupted — not locally and temporarily, but structurally and across an entire generation of organizational life. The concern is not new. The structural basis for it is.

The second objection is optimistic: people rise to the challenge. Leadership capability, on this view, is not primarily a product of conditions — it is a product of character and motivation. This objection rests on a conflation that the previous chapters have worked to distinguish. The capacity to develop judgment is not the same thing as having developed it. And the development of judgment is not primarily a function of motivation or character — it is a function of conditions: of being placed, at the right moments in a career, in situations of genuine complexity, with real stakes, surrounded by feedback. Those conditions can be created deliberately. They can also be allowed to disappear.

The third objection — and perhaps the most genuinely challenging — is that the frame itself is wrong: that what we call "business judgment" is simply the accumulated habits of a particular mode of doing things, and that new modes of doing things will produce different but equally valid forms of capability. This objection contains a real insight. The capacities that future leaders will need are not identical to the capacities that current leaders developed. But the underlying structure of what judgment is — the capacity to relate things, to read situations across multiple registers simultaneously, to decide under conditions of genuine uncertainty — is not changing. And AI is not replacing that capacity: it is bypassing the process through which it is built, while leaving the requirement for it as pressing as it has ever been.

*"The concern is not new. The structural basis for it is."*

# The Vacuum Begins Here

The generation gap that nobody talks about is not a crisis of talent. It is a crisis of conditions. The talent is present — in abundance, and of high quality. What is absent is the developmental infrastructure that has historically converted talent into judgment: the exposure to complexity, the proximity to more experienced practitioners, the feedback loops of consequential uncertainty, the time spent in the difficult space between not knowing and knowing.

The organizations that are beginning to feel this most acutely are not the ones whose people are least capable. They are the ones whose people are technically most sophisticated — and therefore the ones that moved furthest and fastest along the automation curve that removed the formation from the work.

There is nothing to be gained from alarm. The situation is structural, which means it is also addressable — by the same design intelligence that created it, directed toward a different objective. What is needed, before the design work begins, is clarity about what is actually happening: that the pipeline is not filling in the way the pipeline was always understood to fill, that the succession plans of most major organizations rest on an assumption about formation that the conditions of the last two decades have quietly invalidated, and that the timeline for acting is shorter than the comfortable silence around the subject would suggest.

What the vacuum looks like at the level of markets, competitive dynamics, and organizational risk is the subject of the chapters that follow. Before going there, it is worth remaining, for a moment, with the human dimension of what has been described here — because the generation gap is not only an organizational problem. It is a condition that an entire cohort of professionals is living inside, without having been given language for it. They are not failing. They are operating in conditions that were designed for something other than forming them. That is a different problem, with a different set of solutions. And it is a problem that organizations, if they choose to see it clearly, have the capacity to address.


## Notes

1. Elliott Jaques, Requisite Organization: A Total System for Effective Managerial Organization and Managerial Leadership for the 21st Century (Cason Hall, 1989). Jaques's concept of "time-span of discretion" provided a structural framework for understanding organizational hierarchy that has influenced leadership development theory for decades.

2. Grant Thornton, 2024 State of Work in America (November 2024). The survey of 1,500 full-time US employees found that 51 per cent had experienced burnout in the preceding year — a 15 percentage-point increase from the prior year's survey.

3. Aflac, 2024–2025 WorkForces Report (November 2024). The generational breakdown — Millennials at 66%, Gen X at 55%, Boomers at 39% — is drawn from this report's analysis of moderate-to-high burnout experiences across age cohorts.

4. Cariloop, Workplace Burnout in 2025 (2025). The figure of 82% of managers experiencing burnout reflects the specific pressure of the middle management layer.

5. World Health Organization, Burn-out an "Occupational Phenomenon": International Classification of Diseases (ICD-11, May 2019).

6. Thomson Reuters Institute, 2025 Report on the State of the US Legal Market. The shift from 44.5 per cent to 40.2 per cent associate representation, and the corresponding rise in non-equity partnership from 24 per cent to 32 per cent, is drawn from this report's analysis of US law firm composition between 2005 and 2024.

7. Nikia Gray, Executive Director, National Association for Law Placement (NALP), quoted in On The Merits podcast, Bloomberg Law, September 4, 2025.

8. Workforce reduction data drawn from multiple sources: The Logic (July 2025); Fast Company (December 2025); The HR Digest (December 2025).

The figure of 40 per cent decline in non-senior consulting role postings in Canada comes from Indeed data cited in The Logic.

9. ManpowerGroup retirement data cited in Right Management, 'Succession Planning in the Wake of Baby Boomer Retirements' (2024).

10. Challenger, Gray & Christmas, Q1 2025 CEO Turnover Report, cited in VantEdge Search, 'CEO Succession Planning: Fixing the Leadership Pipeline Crisis' (August 2025).

11. VantEdge Search, 'CEO Succession Planning: Fixing the Leadership Pipeline Crisis' (August 2025), with reference to Financial Times analysis of boomerang CEO return performance.

# 5

# When the Last Ones Retire

*What a major knowledge-work organization looks like in 2035 when the judgment-holders are gone.*

It is worth pausing, before we go further, to make the argument concrete.

The preceding chapters have described the judgment vacuum as a structural problem — a generational consequence of the conditions under which professional formation has, for three decades, not occurred. But the vacuum is not a systems abstraction. It is a room full of people in a building somewhere, facing something they cannot quite read, without the resources they need to read it. And the only way to understand it fully is to see it.

What the current chapter attempts is a different register: not analysis, but illustration. A composite scenario, drawn from patterns recognizable to anyone who has spent time at the leadership levels of large organizations, situated in 2035 because that is approximately the horizon at which the current generation of judgment-holders will have, in the main, retired.

The organization is not a specific company. The individuals are not specific people. But the dynamics are real, because they are already beginning.

# The Person Nobody Noticed They Were Losing

Her name, in this scenario, is Elena. She is fifty-eight years old. She has spent the last thirty-two years in the same organization — a global professional services firm with operations in forty countries, forty thousand people, and revenues that place it firmly in the tier that defines the industry. She is not the CEO, or the CFO, or the chief strategy officer. Her title, if you looked her up on the organizational chart, would tell you very little. She is a Managing Director in the client solutions group.

What the organizational chart cannot tell you is what Elena actually does. It cannot tell you that when the CEO is preparing for a difficult board conversation, he has a thirty-minute call with Elena first — not because she is on the governance team, but because she will tell him what is actually going on in the room before he walks into it. It cannot tell you that when two regional leaders have been in low-grade conflict for eighteen months over resource allocation, Elena is the person who eventually sits with each of them separately and finds the language that lets the conflict resolve without anyone losing face. It cannot tell you that she is the person new partners seek out in their first two years, not for formal mentoring, but for the calibration that formal mentoring cannot provide — the real answer to the question: what does it actually take to succeed here, and what does success here actually mean?

Elena built this capacity across three decades of exposure to the organization at every level of complexity it could offer. She started in delivery. She moved through client relationship management at a time when that meant spending three days a week at a client site, absorbing not just what the client needed but how the client's organization worked — its politics, its fears, its informal power structures, its genuine aspirations beneath the stated ones. She managed through a crisis that nearly cost the firm a major client, and learned, through the discomfort of that experience, what the difference was between a relationship that had depth and one that only had history. She spent four years in an emerging market region where the playbook that worked in developed markets did not, and could not, apply.

She is, in the precise sense this book has been building toward, a judgment-holder. Not because she is unusually intelligent — the organization has no shortage of intelligence. Not because she has technical expertise that others lack — the technical expertise in every domain has long since been surpassed by the systems that now handle it. But because she has the accumulated relational and contextual understanding that allows her to read a room, read a situation, read a relationship, and know — not calculate, know — what it requires.[1]

That distinction — between knowing and calculating — is the one that matters most in 2035, because it is the distinction that the preceding decade of AI adoption has sharpened to a point. The organization Elena works for has, by 2035, deployed AI across every domain of its knowledge work: client analytics, delivery management, strategic planning, talent assessment, commercial modeling. The systems are excellent. What they cannot do — what no system trained on historical patterns can do — is read the present moment with the kind of contextual sensitivity that Elena brings to every room she enters. The AI has absorbed the organization's past. Elena understands its present. And that difference, invisible in the data, is precisely what is about to retire.

In 2035, Elena retires. The organization gives her a generous send-off. The CEO's remarks are warm and genuine. And then, quietly, something changes — not in a way that shows up on any dashboard, not in a way that any system flags, not in a way that anyone can immediately name. But it changes. The connective tissue that held certain things together begins, imperceptibly, to loosen.

*"She is, in the precise sense this book has been building toward, a judgment-holder. Not because she is unusually intelligent. But because she has the accumulated*

*relational and contextual understanding that allows her to read a room, read a situation, read a relationship — and know, not calculate, what it requires."*

# The Organization That Looked Fine

In 2035, the firm does not look like an organization in distress. By every conventional measure, it looks like a well-run, technologically sophisticated, operationally excellent enterprise.

The AI systems that underpin its operations are, by the standards of the late 2020s, genuinely impressive. The client analytics platform synthesizes engagement signals across every touch point and produces, in real time, recommendations for relationship management that are more consistent and more data-complete than any human relationship manager could achieve alone. The project delivery system tracks resource allocation, risk signals, and delivery quality across all forty countries, surfacing exceptions before they become problems. The strategic planning process is supported by scenario modeling that draws on a broader range of external data than any previous generation of leaders could have accessed. The outputs are coherent. The dashboards are green.

The leadership team is accomplished. The CEO came up through the strategy practice and has a sharp analytical mind. The CFO is rigorous and technically fluent. The regional leaders are, to a person, hardworking, well-educated, and fluent with the tools available to them.

What is missing does not show up in the dashboards because the dashboards were designed to measure what the organization knows it has. They were not designed to measure what it has quietly lost.

The researcher David DeLong, writing two decades before this moment in a warning that most organizations treated as premature, described what he called the hidden cost of knowledge loss: organizations do not experience it as a shortage, because what leaves with the departing generation is not documented anywhere, cannot be cataloged, and therefore cannot be measured as missing. It simply stops being available.[2] In 2035, that argument has been proven correct at scale.

The most sophisticated measurement systems in the organization track client satisfaction scores, net revenue retention, utilization rates, and employee engagement indices. They do not track — because no one has designed a way to track this — whether the leadership tier has the capacity to make high-stakes decisions under genuine uncertainty. They do not track whether there is anyone in the room, when a complex relational situation arises, who can read what is actually happening beneath the surface of what people are saying. They do not track whether, when the AI surfaces a recommendation, anyone in the room has the formation to know when to follow it and when to override it.

And the person most convinced of the organization's capability — the person who, in every leadership meeting, points to the analytics and describes what they tell the organization with a confidence that fills the room — is the Chief Digital Officer. He is forty-one years old. He has never worked in a role where the AI system was not available. He has never had to navigate a complex client situation without the platform's recommendations. He has simply never built the internalized model that would allow him to know when the system's output is right and when, in some important sense that the system cannot detect, it is not.

## The Crisis That Cannot Be Read

The crisis, when it comes, does not announce itself as one.

It arrives in the form of signals — weak ones at first, then stronger, but never the kind that map cleanly onto the scenarios the strategic planning system has modeled. The firm's largest client in the Asia-Pacific region begins showing what the analytics platform describes as a moderate decline in engagement scores. The platform recommends a set of relationship management interventions: increase contact frequency, schedule a senior executive visit, deploy the client satisfaction recovery protocol. The regional team implements the recommendations. The scores do not recover.

Three months later, a second large client in Europe requests a formal review of the contract terms. The platform flags this as a negotiation risk. The legal and commercial teams prepare the standard response. The presentation is excellent. The client is polite. The contract review stalls.

And then, in the space of six weeks, a third client — a smaller one, but strategically significant — announces that it is consolidating its external relationships and will not be renewing. The announcement comes not via the relationship manager but via a brief, formal letter. No prior signal. No negative engagement score. No flag from the platform.

The executive committee convenes for an emergency session. The slides are prepared. The data is thorough. And then, when the slides run out, something happens that the organization has not quite experienced before: silence.

Not the silence of people thinking. The silence of people who do not know what they are looking at.

The organizational theorist Karl Weick spent decades studying how organizations make sense of situations that do not fit the patterns they know. His work described a specific phenomenon he called the collapse of sense making: the moment at which an organization, confronted with something genuinely novel, loses not just the answer but the capacity to frame the question.[3] Weick gave this experience a phrase — vu jàdé, the opposite of déjà vu: not the comfortable recognition of something seen before, but the disorienting vertigo of something that cannot be placed at all.[4]

The executive committee in 2035 is experiencing vu jàdé. What they are looking at is not a data problem, or a commercial problem, or a technology problem. It is a relationship problem of a kind that has no precedent in their individual experience — because none of them has ever had to navigate a relationship problem of this magnitude without the platform's guidance, and the platform is not equipped to diagnose what is happening here. The problem is not in the engagement scores. It is in something underneath them: a change in how the firm's clients are experiencing the human dimension of the relationship, at a moment when the human beings responsible for that dimension no longer have the formation to understand what the clients are sensing.

Here is what makes this moment categorically different from the crises that the preceding generation navigated. When Elena's cohort faced a client relationship problem of this kind, they had two things that the current leadership team does not: their own formed intuition about what the signals meant, and access to people like Elena, who could read the room and translate what the data was failing to capture. The current leadership team has neither. Their intuition was never built, because the formation that would have built it was absorbed by the AI systems before they had the chance to develop it. And the Elenas of the organization have retired.

The room fills, as it always does in the absence of judgment, with activity. Workstreams are created. A client experience task force is formed. An external consulting firm is retained to conduct a diagnostic — which produces a detailed report that is analytically impeccable and practically inert, because it can only tell the organization what its data shows, not what its data cannot see. None of it is wrong. All of it is insufficient. And the thing that is missing from all of it is the thing the organization no longer has: someone who can walk into the room, listen to what the clients are not saying, and tell the leadership team what is actually going on.

# The Direction Nobody Holds

A pattern emerges in the months that follow which, if you have spent time in organizations at moments of genuine uncertainty, will be familiar. The leadership team cannot agree on what the problem is — and rather than sit with that disagreement, which would require the tolerance for ambiguity that is one of the rarest products of genuine formation, they resolve it the only way available to them: they move.

The strategy shifts, subtly, in the first quarter. Not a reversal — a recalibration. The language around client relationships is sharpened. In the second quarter, the emphasis shifts again: the firm announces a renewed investment in technology-enabled delivery, positioning it as a differentiator rather than a cost measure. In the third quarter, the talent agenda moves to the center: a new program is announced, with external fanfare, promising to develop the next generation of client leaders.

From the outside, each of these moves looks considered. From the inside — experienced by the people three levels below the executive committee who have to translate each new emphasis into their daily work — the effect is something different. It is confusion, accumulating quietly. It is the growing sense that the people at the top do not know which thing to do. It is, at its deepest level, a loss of trust in the organization's capacity to navigate itself.

What drives the oscillation is not indecision in the ordinary sense. It is the absence of the specific capacity that the preceding chapters described: the ability to hold an ambiguous situation open long enough to understand what kind of problem it actually is. The formation that builds that capacity — the repeated experience of being handed a problem with no established methodology, staying with it under pressure, and developing through the discomfort a feel for how to read it — was not part of the career experience of anyone currently in the executive committee.

# The Moment in the Room

There is a scene. It does not happen in the executive committee. It happens in a smaller meeting — a regional leadership review, attended by twelve people who represent the operational core of the firm's largest market.

The numbers are on the table. Revenue is down four percent against the prior year. Client retention is holding, just above the threshold. The regional leader has prepared a thorough analysis: the market is competitive, the pricing environment is challenging, several prospects chose incumbent providers in the last quarter. The CFO representative in the room nods at each explanation, cross-referencing the forecast model.

There is a pause. And then someone says something that nobody in the room quite knows what to do with.

She is not the most senior person present. She has been in the firm for eight years — a significant tenure by the standards of her cohort. She is one of the people who has managed, despite the conditions, to develop some feel for the organization. And what she says is this: *"I don't think the forecast is the problem. I think our people don't believe in where we are going. And I don't think our clients can't feel that."*

A silence settles over the meeting room. Not hostile. Not dismissive. Something more unsettling than either: the silence of people recognizing something they have been aware of but have not had the language for.

The regional leader does not know how to respond, because he does not know whether she is right. Not because the observation is unintelligible — it is entirely intelligible, and he suspects she is describing something real. But because he has no framework for what to do with it. The analytical tools he has been trained to use can tell him what has happened and can model what might happen. They cannot tell him what is true about the human condition of an organization.

After a moment, someone suggests that the people engagement scores be reviewed in the next cycle. Someone else notes that this might be a topic for the upcoming leadership offsite. A third person opens the platform's workforce sentiment module and reads out the current index.

The meeting moves on. The observation is neither addressed nor dismissed. It simply floats — a signal without a receiver, a question without anyone in the room trained to hold it.

This is what the collapse of sense making looks like in a knowledge-work organization in 2035. Not the dramatic unraveling that Weick documented in extremis. Something quieter, and in some ways more dangerous: a leadership team that has excellent tools, excellent data, and no capacity to recognize the category of problem in front of it.

## What Is Actually Absent

The scenario described above is not about failure of intelligence. The people in this organization are not less intelligent than the generation that preceded them. They are, by many conventional measures, more capable: more analytically rigorous, more technically fluent, more globally aware, more comfortable with the tools of modern management. What they are not is formed — not in the specific sense this book has been exploring.

What is absent is the capacity that Weick described as the foundation of organizational sense making: the ability to create order in ambiguous situations by drawing on a deep, internalized understanding of how an organization actually works — its human logics, its relational structures, its informal as well as formal patterns of meaning. That capacity is not a skill that can be trained in a leadership program. It is not a competency that can be assessed in a performance review. It is not an output that an AI system can produce, because it is not produced by processing data — it is produced by living through the experience of an organization across enough of its states and enough of its crises to develop a feel for what it is, as distinct from what it says it is.

Elena had that feel. She had built it across thirty-two years of exposure to the organization in every condition it could offer — growth, contraction, cultural change, client crisis, leadership transition, market disruption. She had been wrong enough times, and had absorbed the consequences of being wrong closely enough, to develop the intuition that is the residue of a thousand corrected errors.

And she is gone. Not because the organization made an error. Not because succession planning failed in any conventional sense. But because the conditions that produced Elena — the formations she passed through, the exposure she accumulated, the feedback she received, the friction she was required to navigate — no longer exist in the organization.

## The Scenario Is Not Inevitable

It is worth being precise about what this scenario is not saying.

It is not saying that the organization will fail. It may not. Organizations are more resilient than their decision-making quality at any given moment would suggest, and the market will not necessarily punish the absence of judgment with the speed and precision that would make the cause visible. The vacuum does not announce itself with a collapse. It announces itself with a drift: a slow, nearly imperceptible erosion of the quality of the decisions that shape the organization's trajectory, visible only in retrospect and only to those with the formation to see it.

It is also not saying that the individuals in this scenario are responsible for their own formation gap. They are not. The conditions that would have formed them were removed before they arrived. The organizations they joined had already made the decisions — the efficiency investments, the automation implementations, the AI adoption strategies — that stripped the developmental texture from the work. They did what capable people do when they are given excellent tools: they used the tools. The atrophy that followed was not a personal failure. It was the structural consequence of designing organizations around the question of what the work needs to produce, without asking what the people doing the work need to develop.

And it is not saying that 2035 is too late. It is not — but the margin is narrowing. The problem is the handover. The problem is what happens the morning after the last Elena retires, when the AI systems are still running perfectly, the dashboards are still green, and the capacity to know what the dashboards are not showing has quietly left the building.

What this chapter is saying — what the scenario is designed to make undeniable — is that the vacuum is real, that its consequences are concrete and organizational rather than abstract and theoretical, and that the time available to address it is shorter than most organizations currently believe.

In that meeting room, when the junior leader said what she said, and the silence settled, and the meeting moved on — something was visible, briefly, to anyone trained to see it. Not a crisis. Not a failure. A gap. The space where the judgment should have been.

It will widen, if nothing changes. That is not a prediction. It is a design consequence.

## Notes

1. Gary Klein's work on Recognition-Primed Decision making — the foundational account of how experts recognize situations rather than calculate responses — is directly applicable here. Klein, Sources of Power: How People

Make Decisions (MIT Press, 1998). The distinction between knowing and calculating is also central to Polanyi's tacit knowledge framework: Polanyi, The Tacit Dimension (Doubleday, 1966).

2. David W. DeLong, Lost Knowledge: Confronting the Threat of an Aging Workforce (Oxford University Press, 2004), p. 4.

3. Karl E. Weick, "The Collapse of Sensemaking in Organizations: The Mann Gulch Disaster," Administrative Science Quarterly 38, no. 4 (1993): 628–652.

4. Weick, "Collapse of Sensemaking," 633. The vu jàdé formulation — "I've never been here before, I have no idea where I am, and I have no idea who can help me" — appears in Weick's analysis of the point at which the smokejumpers lost the cognitive structure required to recognize Dodge's escape fire as a solution rather than an inexplicable act.

# 6

# The Market Consequences

*How judgment scarcity reshapes competitive dynamics, risk, and the nature of strategic advantage at industry level.*

There is a question that sits behind everything this book has argued so far, and it is not a comfortable one: does any of it matter?

The preceding chapters have traced the erosion of a formation process — the apprenticeship chain through which business judgment was historically built — and described how automation, outsourcing, and AI have progressively dismantled it. The argument has been made at the level of organizations: how they lose the capacity to develop the next generation of judgment-holders, how they mistake efficient outputs for formation, how they inherit automated systems without inheriting the reasoning behind them.

But here is the skeptic's counter: organizations are resilient. They absorb losses. They adapt. They find workarounds. Most organizations that face the scenario described in Chapter Five will not visibly collapse. They will drift — making somewhat worse decisions, somewhat more slowly, somewhat less capable of reading what the environment is actually telling them. And in many industries, that drift will not be legibly priced.

So why does it matter at industry level?

It matters for three reasons that are distinct from organizational failure, and each is more insidious than a simple collapse. The first is that when judgment erodes across an entire sector, not just in one firm, it creates a collective blind spot — a category of risk or opportunity that nobody in the industry can see. The second is that judgment scarcity changes the nature of risk itself: not by making individual companies more vulnerable, which it does, but by making systemic risks structurally invisible until the moment they become undeniable. And the third is a paradox that will shape the competitive landscape of the next decade: judgment, precisely because it is becoming scarce, is becoming the most durable source of strategic advantage available — but its scarcity is so poorly understood that most organizations do not yet know they are competing on it.

This chapter examines all three.

## The Convergence Problem: When an Entire Industry Loses the Same Capacity

Consider what happens when most organizations in a sector automate in the same direction. They do not automate randomly — they automate toward efficiency, toward measurability, toward the elimination of variance. The logic is the same across competitors: reduce cost, reduce error, reduce dependence on individual performance. And because the technology available to all of them is roughly the same, and the consulting models that implement it are roughly the same, and the business schools that trained their leaders are roughly the same, they tend to eliminate the same things.

They eliminate the same junior roles. They offshore the same transactional functions. They implement the same ERP platforms and analytical dashboards. And in doing so, they erode judgment in the same places, in the same ways, on roughly the same timescale.

The result is not one organization with a blind spot. It is an entire industry that has lost the capacity to see a particular category of problem — because the formation process that would have produced that capacity has been systematically removed, not by any individual company, but by the logic of competitive imitation applied across all of them.

This is not a theoretical risk. The pattern appears wherever industries have automated intensively in a shared direction. Consider what happened to financial services in the years leading up to 2008. The major institutions had, over the preceding decade, progressively replaced judgment-based risk assessment with model-based risk assessment. The Value at Risk frameworks that became industry standard were built on mathematical assumptions that no individual analyst could easily interrogate or override. The result was not that one bank had a blind spot. Every major institution, having automated risk assessment in the same direction, had the same blind spot: they could not see the category of correlated, systemic risk that was accumulating because their models, built on historical variance, assumed it could not exist.

The Financial Crisis Inquiry Commission later found that major firms and investors had abandoned judgment-based assessment in favor of model outputs, in some cases treating the model as the arbiter of risk and the experienced analyst as redundant. The CEO of Citigroup acknowledged that a multi-billion position in highly rated mortgage securities would not, at the time, have attracted his attention.[1] What he was describing was not individual failure. It was the collective consequence of an industry that had automated judgment out of risk assessment — and then discovered that the risks the models could not see were the ones that mattered most.

More recently, the Financial Stability Board warned in its 2024 report on the financial stability implications of AI that the widespread adoption of similar AI models and data sources by competing institutions could produce dangerous market correlations — situations in which different banks, directed by systems trained on the same data, make identical decisions simultaneously under conditions of stress, amplifying volatility rather than absorbing it.[2] The FSB called this the herding effect. It is, at root, a judgment problem: when the institutions responsible for reading and pricing risk have delegated that reading to systems that share the same assumptions, the diversity of perspective that markets depend on for stability disappears.

The physical mechanism behind this is worth pausing on. For decades, London taxi drivers who qualified under the city's legendary licensing system — a two-to-four year process of memorizing 25,000 streets and 20,000 landmarks known simply as The Knowledge — were found to have measurably larger hippocampi than the general population.[3] The brain structure most associated with spatial memory and cognitive mapping had physically developed in response to the demands placed on it. The formation built the capacity. When GPS arrived and the navigational demands disappeared, the reverse pattern emerged: the cognitive capacity atrophied through disuse. The tool did not supplement the capacity. It replaced it.

Now apply that mechanism across an entire industry. When every competitor in a sector deploys the same analytical tools to handle the same categories of judgment, the human capacity those tools were designed to assist atrophies. Not at the individual level only, but at the industry level. The cognitive map that a well-formed senior leader once carried is no longer being built by anyone. And when an entire industry has lost that capacity, the thing it can no longer see is not randomly distributed — it is systematically the thing the tools were not designed to measure.

# Two Categories of Risk: Why the Dangerous One Is Invisible

Not all risk is equal in its relationship to judgment. The first category is operational and compliance risk: adherence to regulation, statutory reporting, legal obligations, misconduct prevention, process integrity. This category is broadly amenable to systematic management. It can be defined, measured, audited, and enforced. Organizations have become, in many respects, genuinely better at managing this category over the past two decades — more consistent, more comprehensive, less dependent on whether any individual happened to notice something.

The second category is different in kind. This is strategic and contextual risk: the risk that market signals are being misread, that a competitor's behavior is signaling something your pricing model is not capturing, that an employee mood shift is a leading indicator of retention failure, that a geopolitical development three steps removed from your supply chain is about to become an operational constraint. These risks are not on any checklist. They cannot be automated into a monitoring system, because they do not exist as discrete events — they exist as patterns, relationships, and accumulating tendencies that are only legible to someone with the formation to read them.

Judgment scarcity matters almost not at all to the first category of risk. What judgment scarcity does is hollow out the organizational capacity to manage the second category — and it does so gradually, invisibly, in ways that produce no immediate signal.

The consequences of second-category risk failures do not surface immediately. They surface eventually, and when they surface, they tend to surface as crises that appear to come from nowhere — sudden reputation collapses, strategic pivots that seemed rational but left the organization structurally exposed, market position erosion that happened, in retrospect, over several years of accumulated misreading. The organization that faces this kind of failure rarely knows it has been failing. The dashboard looked fine. The compliance reports were clean. What was not on any report was the slow atrophying of the human capacity to read what the environment was actually signaling.

This is why the standard organizational resilience framework, which tends to focus on the capacity to respond to visible shocks, is an incomplete description of the risk that judgment scarcity creates. The more dangerous exposure is not to shock — it is to drift. Organizations, like ecosystems, can tolerate considerable drift before the degradation becomes visible. But the drift accumulates. And when the shock eventually comes — the moment of genuine environmental discontinuity that requires the organization to navigate by something more than the last known pattern — the human capacity to navigate may no longer be there.

## The Measurement Paradox: Why the Most Valuable Asset Is Not Being Counted

In a striking proportion of science fiction stories — across cultures, across decades, across genres — when the storyteller needs to represent the highest form of collective wisdom, they reach for the same image: a circular council of elders. Grey-haired, unhurried, seated in a ring that implies no hierarchy above the group itself. The image recurs in Frank Herbert, in Ursula Le Guin, in dozens of fictional societies imagined by writers who had no particular reason to converge on the same picture. What they were encoding, perhaps without articulating it explicitly, is the intuition that the deepest form of judgment is accumulated, embodied, and irreplaceable — that it cannot be delegated to youth or transferred through instruction, that it lives in people who have been through enough to know what they are seeing. The storytelling instinct understood something that organizational design has not yet built an instrument to measure. This chapter is about the consequences of that gap.

Here is the paradox at the heart of the competitive argument. If judgment is becoming scarce, and if scarcity drives value in functioning markets, then judgment should be becoming more valuable. The organizations that have retained it should be building a latent competitive advantage that will compound over time.

The strategic logic is straightforward. Jay Barney's resource-based view of the firm argues that sustainable competitive advantage derives from resources that are valuable, rare, inimitable, and non-substitutable.[4] Judgment, understood correctly, satisfies all four conditions. It is valuable — it produces better decisions under conditions of ambiguity and novelty. It is rare — its formation conditions have been systematically dismantled across most organizations. It is inimitable — it cannot be purchased or replicated from outside; it must be formed through particular developmental experiences over time. And it is non-substitutable — AI systems can process data and generate recommendations, but they cannot replace the contextual, embodied, socially-formed capacity to make sense of situations for which there is no precedent.

The problem is the measurement paradox. Judgment does not appear on a balance sheet. It is not captured in any standard performance metric. It only reveals itself under discontinuity — in the moments when the environment presents something the models were not trained for, and the organization must navigate by something else.

This creates a specific failure mode worth naming precisely. Organizations still believe they are recognizing and rewarding judgment through the traditional promotion ladder. But what the preceding chapters have established is that this assumption is no longer reliable. The accelerating displacement of cognitive work by AI means that the conditions through which that maturity was historically built are no longer part of most people's developmental path. The promotion is being granted. The judgment is not being formed.

And so organizations are promoting into senior roles people who hold the designation of judgment without having gone through the formation. The gap is not visible in performance reviews. It is not visible in the dashboard. It is not visible until the moment of genuine environmental stress — and by that point, the gap has been compounding, undetected, for years.

What makes this a market-level problem, not just an organizational one, is that the gap is distributed across sectors. If the failure were concentrated — if one company had clearly hollow leadership while its competitors retained depth — the market would, over time, punish it. But when the erosion is distributed — when most organizations in a sector have been forming their leadership pipeline through the same hollow process — the competitive reference point is itself compromised. There is no obvious benchmark of superior judgment performance against which to measure the degradation, because the degradation is everywhere.

## The Fragmentation of Judgment: Depth Without Breadth

What automation and outsourcing have produced, across the decades, is not so much the absence of judgment as its fragmentation. The offshore team that took over transactional processing developed deep judgment at process engineering problems. The retained onshore function developed judgment at client relationship management. The analytics team developed judgment at data interpretation. Each of these is a genuine form of judgment. Each is valuable in its domain.

But the organizational capacity that is disappearing is something different from any of them: it is the integrative judgment that sits above the domains, that can move across them, that can read the relationship between a process failure and a client sentiment and a competitive signal and a regulatory development and synthesize them into a coherent assessment of what the organization should do. That integrative capacity was built, historically, through the kind of career path that no longer exists for most people entering organizations today — the path that moved a person across functions, across geographies, across cycles of growth and contraction and crisis and recovery.

AI will accelerate this fragmentation further. Where previous waves removed the conditions for forming operational judgment, AI removes the conditions for forming reasoning itself. The person who uses AI to draft, to analyze, to synthesize, to evaluate options, is not developing the analytical muscles that those activities would have built. They are developing the muscle of directing AI — which is a real and valuable capability, but it is not the same thing as the capacity to reason under pressure when the AI's outputs are inadequate or simply wrong.

The research on cognitive offloading consistently finds the same mechanism: when a cognitive function is systematically offloaded to a tool, the underlying human capacity for that function declines — not through any failure of the individual, but through the straightforward logic of use-dependency. The 2022 PISA assessment found the largest global decline in student performance since the test's creation, and researchers noted that downward trends were already evident before the pandemic disruptions, pointing to structural drivers rather than transient ones.[5]

## The Strategic Opportunity in Scarcity

There is, in all of this, a competitive signal that has not yet been widely read — and that is precisely what makes it valuable.

The organizations that are now building deliberate formation infrastructure — that are designing roles and careers to develop integrative judgment, that are creating the conditions of friction, feedback, and lateral exposure that build the capacity to reason across discontinuity — are not, by conventional metrics, the most efficient. They are accepting some degree of redundancy, some degree of role overlap, some deliberate slowing of the automated throughput in order to preserve the developmental conditions that efficiency would otherwise eliminate. They look, by the measures currently in use, marginally less optimized than their competitors.

But they are accumulating, silently, the resource that will matter most when the next discontinuity arrives. And discontinuities always arrive.

The competitive advantage that judgment creates is not evenly distributed through time. It concentrates at the moments of maximum environmental uncertainty — the crises, the pivots, the moments of genuine novelty when the models stop working and the organization must navigate by something else. At those moments, the organization with a depth of formed judgment has a decisive and structural advantage. Not because its systems are better. But because its people can read what the systems cannot, and can act on what they read.

The paradox of the current moment is that the organizations most likely to have retained this capacity are also the organizations least likely to know they have it — because they have not had a language for what they have preserved, and they have not had a metric for measuring its value. They have kept some things that efficiency models said should be cut, for reasons that felt intuitively right but were hard to defend in a business case.

This is the competitive signal that is not yet in the market. The organizations that can build that language, develop that metric, and make deliberate what has so far been accidental — those organizations are not building a competitive advantage. They are building the only sustainable one available as the efficiency frontier converges.

Because at the efficiency frontier, there is no competitive advantage in efficiency. When every competitor has access to the same AI tools, the same automation platforms, the same analytical infrastructure, the marginal gain from further automation approaches zero. What remains, at that frontier, is the capacity that cannot be automated: the judgment to understand what the tools are missing, the formation to navigate what the tools cannot navigate, and the organizational design to keep producing that capacity in successive generations of leaders.

That is the market consequence of judgment scarcity. Not just risk and exposure — though those are real. But a competitive landscape in which the organizations that have understood what they were losing, and designed deliberately to replace it, are building the most defensible position available.

The question, which the final moments of this book will address, is how.

## Notes

1. Financial Crisis Inquiry Commission, The Financial Crisis Inquiry Report (Washington, DC: US Government Printing Office, 2011). The Commission's findings document the industry-wide displacement of judgment by model outputs in risk assessment.

2. Financial Stability Board, The Financial Stability Implications of Artificial Intelligence (FSB, November 2024). The report identified market correlations as a primary systemic vulnerability arising from the widespread adoption of similar AI models across competing institutions.

3. Eleanor A. Maguire et al., 'Navigation-Related Structural Change in the Hippocampi of Taxi Drivers,' Proceedings of the National Academy of Sciences 97, no. 8 (2000): 4398–4403. The study found that the posterior hippocampi of London taxi drivers who had qualified under The Knowledge were significantly larger than those of matched controls, and that hippocampal volume correlated with time spent as a cab driver.

4. Jay B. Barney, 'Firm Resources and Sustained Competitive Advantage,' Journal of Management 17, no. 1 (1991): 99–120.

5. The 2022 PISA (Program for International Student Assessment) results, published by the OECD, recorded the largest single-cycle decline in measured performance since the assessment's creation in 2000. The OECD noted

that downward trends were discernible before the COVID-19 pandemic, indicating structural rather than purely situational drivers.

# 7

# What Machines Cannot Inherit



*Moment III — The Human Reframe*

*The specific nature of judgment — contextual, embodied, accumulated — and why it cannot be engineered into existence.*

There is a version of this chapter that would be easy to write, and wrong.

It would begin with a list of things humans do that AI cannot — empathy, creativity, moral reasoning — and build toward a reassuring conclusion: that in the competition between human and machine, the human wins on the dimensions that matter most. It would be comforting. It would also be dishonest, because it would be making a claim about permanence that cannot be sustained, and because it would be drawing the wrong kind of line in the wrong place for the wrong reasons.

That is not the argument here.

The argument here is more precise — and ultimately more useful — than a defensive perimeter around human uniqueness. It is this: judgment, as this book has defined it, is not a capability that humans possess and machines lack. It is a capability that is produced by a specific kind of formation

— accumulated through exposure, consequence, relational trust, and the particular friction of being responsible for outcomes that matter to real people in real time. And that formation process is not something AI can replicate, not because AI is insufficiently sophisticated, but because the formation is constitutively human. It requires a kind of skin in the game that no system can have.

This distinction matters enormously, because it changes what the problem actually is. The question is not whether AI will eventually match human judgment on some abstract capability scale. The question is whether organizations will continue to create the conditions under which judgment is formed in human beings — and what happens when they don't.

By the time most readers encounter this argument, they will have had conversations with AI systems that felt, at moments, almost uncannily perceptive. Systems that tracked emotional register, adapted their tone, surfaced relevant context, and offered responses that a junior analyst in most organizations could not have matched. That experience is real, and dismissing it as mere simulation would be intellectually dishonest. The sophistication is genuine. But sophistication is not the same as formation. And the gap between them is precisely the gap this chapter is about.

## What Judgment Actually Is

To understand why judgment cannot be engineered, it helps to be precise about what judgment actually is — not the colloquial version, but the operational one.

Judgment, as it appears in this book, is not the application of expertise. Expertise is domain-specific and largely codifiable — the kind of deep pattern-recognition that operates in high-validity environments, where feedback is reliable and the patterns learned over time are genuinely predictive of the patterns that will appear tomorrow. A chess grandmaster has expertise. A skilled radiologist has expertise. In high-validity environments, AI systems are already competitive with human expertise, and will become more so.

Judgment operates in a different register. It is what you exercise when the environment is not high-validity — when the patterns are ambiguous, when the feedback is delayed or indirect, when the stakes are relational rather than technical[1], when the variables include not just information but the people who hold it, interpret it, and will have to live with the consequences of what is decided. Judgment is what bridges expertise to action in conditions where expertise alone is insufficient.

Consider what distinguishes these two registers in practice. An analyst with expertise in financial modeling can build a model that accurately represents the available data. A leader with judgment knows which assumptions the model is concealing, which stakeholders will interpret it in ways that serve their interests rather than the organization's, and what the model cannot say about the moment in which the decision will land. The expertise produces the analysis. The judgment determines what the analysis means — and what to do with it.

That second capacity — the one that determines meaning — is what judgment-holders carry, and what organizations lose when they leave. And it is built not through the accumulation of information, but through the accumulation of experience: the repeated encounter with consequential uncertainty, with the friction of being responsible for outcomes, with the gradual calibration of pattern-recognition against the reality of how organizations actually behave when the pressure is on.

---

[1]

# The Formation That Cannot Be Shortcut

There is a story from the delivery of a large-scale offshore transition that illustrates the point with unusual precision — though the specifics matter less than what they reveal.

The scenario: a major organizational restructuring, moving hundreds of senior roles across geographies in half the planned time. The metrics, when examined, showed nothing alarming. Delivery performance was within tolerance. Engagement surveys returned no clear signal. But two things were happening that the data could not see: attrition was running at nearly seven times its normal rate, and senior stakeholders across the globe were escalating concerns with unusual frequency. The system said: nothing is wrong. The situation said: something is critically wrong.

The response was not analytical. It was relational. Two things happened. First: direct, personal phone calls to senior stakeholders — not emails, not formal communications, not structured feedback sessions. One-to-one conversations, initiated without agenda, with the explicit purpose of making a human being available where a process had previously been visible. Second: months of informal, face-to-face time with the team — not surveys, not HR frameworks, not structured listening exercises. Conversations. The kind in which people tell you what is actually happening when they are not being evaluated for saying it.

Within months, attrition normalized. Escalations disappeared. Nothing structural had changed. What had changed was the relational architecture — the network of trust and visibility that allowed people to know who was responsible, who was listening, and where the safety net was. The data had not seen the problem. The relationship found it. And the relationship could only be built by someone who understood — not analytically, but through accumulated experience — what the data was failing to capture and what kind of human contact would restore what the acceleration had damaged.

This is what judgment does. The capacity deployed was not knowledge of a domain. It was knowledge of how people behave under pressure, what trust requires, what the absence of visible leadership does to a team that is already uncertain, and what kind of conversation creates enough safety for the truth to emerge. That knowledge was not in any system. It was accumulated across years of exposure to exactly the kind of organizational complexity that produces it.

The question is whether that formation process is replicable at the system level — whether AI can be trained on enough examples of this kind of judgment to eventually produce it. And the answer, considered precisely, is no. Not because the examples are insufficient, but because judgment of this kind is not a pattern that can be extracted from outcomes. It is a capacity that is built through the process of being responsible for outcomes — through the felt experience of consequence, of recovery, of relationship, of trust earned and trust lost and trust rebuilt. The formation is not the input to the capability. The formation is the capability.

## The Structural Ceiling

This is the point at which technically sophisticated readers will push back, and the push back deserves a direct answer.

The objection runs something like this: AI systems are advancing rapidly in exactly the dimensions being described. They read emotional register. They adapt to context. They model relationships and institutional dynamics with increasing sophistication. Why is the gap described here permanent rather than temporary?

The honest answer begins with a concession: it is not permanent in the way a physical law is permanent. AI systems will continue to improve. Some of what is described here as judgment will, over time, be approximated more closely by systems trained on richer data with more sophisticated models.

That is not in dispute.

But the concession does not undermine the argument. It clarifies it. Because the argument is not that AI cannot simulate the outputs of judgment. It is that AI cannot undergo the formation that produces it. And formation — in the precise sense this book has been building toward — is not a function of training data. It is a function of consequence.

An AI system trained on thousands of examples of the offshore transition scenario described above would, in time, learn to recommend relational interventions. What it cannot do is have been responsible for the outcome. It cannot have experienced the weight of a team depending on a decision it made. It cannot have rebuilt trust with a stakeholder who had reason not to extend it. It cannot have been wrong in a way that cost something real, and learned from that cost at the level of embodied calibration — the kind of learning that happens not in a model update but in the integration of experience into a self that carries the consequence forward.

This is not a romantic distinction. It is a structural one. The skin in the game that produces judgment is not a metaphor for commitment or seriousness. It is a description of the feedback mechanism through which judgment is actually built. You cannot simulate having stakes. And without stakes, you cannot produce the kind of formation that creates a judgment-holder.

There is a deeper structural point that goes beyond the individual. AI systems are trained on aggregated historical patterns. What they optimize for, at root, is a kind of calibrated average of past behavior in analogous situations. Judgment, as this book has defined it, is precisely the capacity to identify when the present situation is not analogous to past patterns — when the model is wrong, when the consensus is based on shared assumptions that no longer apply, when the room contains something that the data cannot see. The capacity to know when the system is failing requires standing outside the system. And that position — the position of the person who has accumulated enough contextual, relational, consequence-bearing experience to see what the model misses — is not a position that AI can occupy. By design, it is inside the model.

## The Spark That Data Cannot Ignite

In the organizations built during the efficiency era — the ones designed for precision, measurability, and the elimination of variance — something happened to the humans inside them that was not an intended consequence of the design. They were taken out of the decisions. Not all at once, and not completely, but progressively: their judgment was replaced by process, their discretion was bounded by policy, their creativity was redirected toward execution within pre-defined parameters. The job description replaced the person.

The consequence was not, primarily, a loss of judgment — though it was that. The consequence was a loss of the conditions under which people bring what is most valuable in them to their work. There is something visible in the moment when a person is genuinely included in a consequential decision — not consulted in the performative sense, but actually brought into the space of uncertainty and asked to help navigate it. The response is not compliance. It is something qualitatively different: a kind of activation that produces insight, commitment, and the particular quality of attention that only comes from genuine stakes.

This is not a philosophical observation about human dignity, though it is consistent with one. It is an organizational observation about what produces value. The organizations that are already navigating the judgment vacuum most effectively are not the ones that have retained the most human judgment-holders by accident. They are the ones that have, whether deliberately or intuitively, continued to create conditions under which people encounter consequential complexity, are held responsible for navigating it, and are given enough space — enough protected uncertainty — that the formation continues. These organizations are not resisting automation. They are designing around it, creating the friction that the automated layer has removed.

Decentralization — in the precise organizational sense, not the political one — is part of this design. The organizations most vulnerable to the judgment vacuum are the ones that have concentrated decision-making at the top and automated everything below, creating a structure in which the only remaining judgment is held by the people closest to retirement. The organizations that are building judgment systematically are the ones that have distributed consequential responsibility down through the hierarchy — creating the conditions, at every level, for the kind of encounters with complexity and consequence that produce formation.

This is not a rejection of leadership. It is a redesign of what leadership is for. The job of the senior leader in this model is not to hold the judgment and dispense decisions. It is to create the conditions under which judgment develops in others — to be, in a very precise sense, the architect of formation rather than the repository of it.

## Why This Is the Hope Argument

It would be possible to read everything in this chapter as a lament — a description of what is being lost, framed slightly differently than the chapters that preceded it. That reading would miss the point.

The argument being made here is not that human judgment is precious and fragile and under threat. It is that human judgment is structurally irreproducible by the systems that are replacing it — and that this structural fact, properly understood, is the most important competitive insight available to any organization operating in the current environment. The scarcity is real. The advantage it creates is real. And the path to capturing that advantage is not a retreat from technology but a deliberate redesign of the conditions under which human formation occurs alongside it.

The organizations that will define competitive advantage in the next decade are not the ones that have the most sophisticated AI. Every organization will have sophisticated AI — it will be a commodity input, as fundamental and as undifferentiating as electricity. The organizations that will lead are the ones that have figured out how to use AI as the infrastructure that frees humans to do the thing AI cannot do: accumulate judgment, build relational trust, navigate the ambiguity that lies beyond the model's edge, and make the decisions that require not a calculation but a person.

The round table, rather than the hierarchy with its apex. Not because it is a more egalitarian arrangement, though it may be. Because it is a more intelligent one. The judgment that any organization needs is distributed through its people — accumulated through their varied exposures, their different contexts, their particular histories of consequence and recovery. A structure that concentrates decision-making at the top squanders that distribution. A structure that creates the conditions for judgment to develop, and be exercised, at every level of complexity the organization contains — that is the structure that will be most capable of reading what the environment is actually telling it, at the moment when that reading matters most.

That is what machines cannot inherit. Not a feeling. Not a soul. Not a uniquely human essence that resists technological encroachment. But the accumulated, consequence-bearing, relationally embedded capacity that is produced by a specific kind of formation — and that no system, however sophisticated, can produce on its own behalf.

The question for the chapters that follow is what it takes to build it back — deliberately, structurally, and at scale.

**Notes**

1. Daniel Kahneman and Gary Klein, 'Conditions for intuitive expertise: a failure to disagree,' American Psychologist 64, no. 6 (2009): 515–526.

# 8

# The New Human Premium

*How the scarcity of judgment changes the economics of talent, leadership, and organizational value — and what it actually looks like when an organization begins to price what it has always taken for granted.*

There is a person in almost every organization who occupies a space that no chart can represent. Not because she is senior — she may not be the most senior person in the room. Not because of her technical expertise — others may be more analytically precise. But when she speaks, the conversation changes register. When she is absent from a meeting, something indeterminate but important is missing. When she leaves the organization, people say, in the weeks and months after: I don't know why, but things feel different now.

This person is not unusual. She has existed in every organization that has functioned at any level of complexity for any sustained period of time. What is unusual — what is new — is the direction of travel. The conditions that produced her are being dismantled. The pipeline that would have produced the person who comes after her has been, as the preceding chapters have established, systematically thinned. And the gap between her value and the organization's understanding of that value has never been wider.

Chapter 7 made the structural case: judgment of this kind is irreproducible by AI systems not because those systems lack sophistication, but because the formation process that produces judgment — the accumulated, consequence-bearing, relationally embedded experience of navigating complexity with real stakes — is not a process that can be shortcut, simulated, or delegated to a system. The formation is the capability.

This chapter asks what follows from that. If judgment is genuinely scarce, and if scarcity in functioning markets produces value, then judgment is becoming the most economically significant organizational asset of the coming decade. That claim requires unpacking — because the economics of judgment do not behave like the economics of other assets, because organizations are systematically misreading the signals, and because the talent market inversion that scarcity implies is only beginning to make itself visible.

## The Maestro and the Orchestra

There is a useful analogy for what the human premium actually consists of, and it is not the one that usually gets reached for.

The standard framing of the "human advantage" in an AI era tends toward a list of soft qualities: empathy, creativity, emotional intelligence, ethical reasoning. These are real capabilities, and they matter. But they are not, by themselves, precise enough to carry an economic argument. Empathy without formation is warmth. Creativity without judgment is noise. The qualities need a structural framework before they can become a strategic claim.

The more precise image is the conductor. Every instrument in an orchestra is specialized — the oboist has spent a decade mastering a domain that the violinist cannot approximate. Every player, in isolation, is technically accomplished. What the conductor brings is not additional technical skill in any instrument. It is something categorically different: the capacity to hold the entire structure in mind simultaneously — to read the relationship between the cello line and the trumpet entrance, to sense when the rhythm is pulling against the emotional arc of the movement, to make real-time adjustments that no individual player can make because no individual player can hear what the conductor hears.

That integrative capacity — the ability to hold multiple registers at once and act across them — is precisely what the preceding chapters have established as the disappearing organizational capability. And it is the core of what the human premium consists of.

But the conductor analogy contains a second, less obvious implication that is equally important for what follows. The conductor is not merely integrating specialists. She is orchestrating a relationship between human judgment and structured execution — between the parts of the performance that are practiced, repeatable, and technically determined, and the parts that are live, relational, and require real-time reading of the room. This is the organizational design of the AI era in compressed form. AI is an extraordinary instrument. It is, in certain dimensions, the most powerful instrument in the ensemble. What it cannot do is conduct itself.

This matters because it reframes the question of what organizations will need from their most valuable humans. The premium is not simply for people who can do things AI cannot. It is for people who can do the conductor's job: who can orchestrate the relationship between AI's extraordinary processing capacity and the human judgment that determines what that capacity is pointed at, what its outputs mean, and what to do when they are wrong. That is an integrative, relational, contextual capability. And it is, in the precise sense established throughout this book, a formation-dependent one. It cannot be acquired by taking a course. It is accumulated through exactly the kinds of consequential exposure that the efficiency era and the AI era have been systematically removing.

# What Scarcity Does to Value

The economic logic of scarcity is familiar enough in markets that can price what they are buying. When a resource is valuable and becoming rare, its price rises. The organizations that retain it gain a structural advantage. The talent market adjusts. The advantage compounds.

What makes judgment different is that this logic is operating in a market that cannot yet name what it is pricing. The signals are there — but they are informal, indirect, and often misread by the organizations that encounter them.

The pattern is visible, once you know what to look for. It appears in the meeting where a specific person is invited regardless of whether their functional role should place them there — where their presence is felt to be load-bearing in a way that resists explanation by org chart logic. It appears in client relationships, where a particular individual becomes the reason a client stays: not the team, not the product, not the deliverable, but the person — her ability to read the situation, to know when the conversation needs to shift register, to hold the relationship through difficulty in a way that no system can replicate and no process can mandate. It appears in executive hiring, where boards reach for candidates whose most important quality is described in terms that resist the competency framework: someone who has "seen a lot," who "gets it," who "knows how organizations actually work." These are imprecise descriptions of something quite precise: the accumulated contextual judgment that is formed through consequence.

The Russell Reynolds Leadership Confidence Index, now in its fifth year, provides some of the clearest quantitative evidence that this pressure is beginning to emerge at the senior levels of organizations. CEO confidence in their C-suite has declined across almost every dimension — but the steepest fall, and the most revealing, is in succession planning. Confidence in leadership succession dropped to 50.5 in 2025, continuing a sustained decline from 2021, and only 36 per cent of CEOs report having a successful C-suite succession strategy, down from 45 per cent in 2022. Fewer than half of board directors believe their CEO succession plans will succeed.[1] That is not a crisis of process. Succession processes have never been more elaborate. It is a crisis of pipeline — the recognition, surfacing slowly and uncomfortably into the awareness of boards and CEOs, that the talent behind the current leadership tier does not contain what they expected it to contain.

The same report found that fewer than half of CEOs believe their organizations have the forward-thinking leadership needed to align resources for AI effectively — despite 65 per cent being excited about AI's potential and 83 per cent optimistic about productivity gains. The gap between ambition and execution is, at root, a judgment gap. The tools are available. The formation to direct them is not.

This is what the early market signal for the human premium looks like. It does not arrive as a price discovery event — a moment when organizations explicitly decide to pay more for judgment. It arrives as a slow, uncomfortable recognition that something critical is absent in the people who should by now be ready to lead — and a search for language to describe what that thing is.

## The Inversion That Is Coming

For two decades, the talent market rewarded a specific configuration of capability: technical sophistication married to analytical precision. Data fluency, systems literacy, quantitative rigor. These were genuine scarce skills in a world where organizations were building out their analytical and digital infrastructure, and the market priced them accordingly. The analyst who could model, the engineer who could build, the consultant who could frame a quantitative business case — these were the profiles that organizations competed for, compensated at premium rates, and promoted on a fast track.

That configuration is about to invert. Not overnight, and not completely — technical fluency will remain necessary. But it will no longer be sufficient, and more importantly, it will no longer be scarce. AI systems can now do much of what the technical expert spent a decade learning to do. Not everything — and not without direction. But enough that the skill that was previously the differentiator is now becoming the baseline, available at scale to any organization that can direct it.

What does not commoditize is the formation-dependent layer: the capacity to read a room that hasn't been read before, to hold a relationship through a crisis that has no precedent, to make a judgment call in a genuinely novel situation where the models offer no clear answer. These are capabilities that take time to build, require specific kinds of developmental exposure, and cannot be purchased or replicated from the outside. In the terms of Jay Barney's resource-based view of the firm, they satisfy all four conditions for durable competitive advantage: they are valuable, rare, inimitable, and non-substitutable.[2] The scarcity is structural, not contingent. It will not be resolved by a better training program.

The evidence that this inversion is underway is still more signal than proof — more pattern than data. But the pattern is consistent. It is visible in the boomerang CEO phenomenon documented in Chapter 4, where boards reach backward for a previous leader precisely because the person they need is not in the pipeline they built. It is visible in the "crucible experiences" language that Russell Reynolds uses to describe what transformationally capable leaders have that others lack — not credentials, not competency ratings, but specific encounters with high-stakes complexity that produce a kind of formation no program can replicate.[3]

Medicine offers a clarifying parallel. Medical training has driven toward specialization for three decades. The logic is correct in its own terms: a specialist who has spent ten thousand hours on a specific pathology is genuinely more capable within that domain than a generalist. The efficiency gain is real. But the consequence has been a quiet erosion of something that patients feel acutely: the capacity of the clinical encounter to be genuinely human. UK GPs, constrained to an average consultation time of under ten minutes — among the shortest in Europe — deliver excellent diagnostic precision in an encounter that many patients experience as depersonalized. [4] The clinical output is technically sound. What has been optimized away is the relational capacity to accompany a patient: to read not just the presenting symptom but the fear behind it, to hold space for the uncertainty that no diagnostic algorithm can fully address, to provide the kind of human contact that is itself therapeutic.

What AI will do to medicine is make the technical layer — diagnosis, treatment selection, drug interaction analysis, predictive risk assessment — more powerful than any individual clinician can achieve. What AI cannot do is be present to a patient who is frightened. The doctor's role does not disappear. But it transforms into something closer to what medicine was always meant to be: the clinical encounter as an act of human accompaniment, enabled by AI's technical depth and distinguished by a specifically human capacity to be there.

The organizational parallel is precise. The analyst who builds the model and the consultant who frames the business case are the diagnostic specialists. They will be augmented — and increasingly, replaced at the execution layer — by AI systems of extraordinary capability. What organizations will need, and will struggle to find, are the people who can do what the conductor does and what the physician should do: who bring not processing power but presence, not breadth of information but depth of formation, not the capacity to produce an answer but the capacity to know what the answer means and what it will take to act on it.

*"The premium is not for people who can do what AI cannot. It is for people who can do the conductor's job — orchestrating the relationship between AI's processing power and the judgment that determines what that power is for."*

## The Measurement Problem — Again

Here is where the economic argument encounters its most stubborn obstacle, and it is the same obstacle encountered throughout this book: the thing that is becoming most valuable is the thing that is hardest to measure.

Standard financial accounting prohibits internally developed knowledge and organizational capital from appearing on a firm's balance sheet.[5] A patent, once acquired through a transaction, can be valued and recorded. The judgment of a Managing Director who has spent thirty years building the relational and contextual understanding that makes her uniquely capable of navigating the organization's most complex challenges — that appears nowhere. It is not an asset in any standard sense. And what does not appear as an asset does not, in most organizations, get protected, developed, or priced with any precision.

As of 2020, intangible assets represented approximately 90 per cent of the total value of S&P 500 companies, against only 17 per cent in 1975.[6] The economy has been running on intangibles for decades. Most of those intangibles — brand, customer relationships, organizational knowledge — are understood to be valuable even if they resist precise measurement. Judgment, as described in this book, is the most intangible of intangibles. It does not show up in engagement scores, competency ratings, or leadership program completions. It shows up in outcomes — in the decisions that held under pressure, in the relationships that survived complexity, in the crises that were navigated rather than managed. And outcomes, in most organizations, are attributed to the system, the strategy, or the process — not to the person who held the whole thing together.

This creates a specific failure mode with an almost mechanical character. Organizations believe they are recognizing and rewarding judgment through the performance management system. Annual objectives are set, performance is assessed against them, and variable compensation is allocated accordingly. The process generates enormous internal tension — not because it is dishonest, but because it is structurally incapable of capturing the most important thing. Individual goals, however carefully constructed, fragment the collective: each person optimizes for their measured contribution to the whole, in ways that systematically undervalue the integrative capacity that makes the whole more than the sum of its parts. The conductor's contribution cannot be measured by looking at any individual instrument. The performance management system was not designed to measure the conductor.

The consequence is a distortion in how organizations value their people that compounds over time. The profiles that the measurement system can capture — the technically precise, the analytically productive, the consistently goal-achieving — tend to rise. The profiles that the measurement system cannot capture — the integrative, the relationally sophisticated, the genuinely formative in their effects on others — tend to be seen but not counted, valued but not protected, until they leave and the value becomes visible in its absence. Elena, in Chapter 5, was not underpaid. She was mis-valued — in the specific sense that the measurement system had no instrument for the asset she represented.

## Leadership Swings and the Elena Problem

There is a further structural dynamic that operates in parallel with the measurement failure, and it deserves acknowledgment because it is both pervasive and rarely named directly.

Organizations do not have consistent leadership philosophies. They cycle. A period of hierarchical, results-driven, efficiency-focused leadership is followed by a period of more collaborative, values-led, stakeholder-sensitive leadership — and then, often, back again. Each cycle rewards certain profiles and sidelines others. The people who thrive over long careers are not necessarily the most capable; they are often the most adaptable — those who can read the current cycle and align themselves to it sufficiently to maintain organizational relevance.

Elena — the profile described in Chapter 5, the person nobody noticed they were losing until she was gone — was precisely the kind of person who could navigate these cycles. She had built enough organizational knowledge, enough relational depth, enough contextual wisdom that her value was visible across different leadership philosophies and different organizational climates. The friction she had accumulated over three decades had produced a kind of organizational suppleness — the capacity to be genuinely useful in a wide range of conditions, not just the ones her current role was optimized for.

But here is the problem that the current moment intensifies. When leadership cycles swing sharply — when the philosophy changes with sufficient force and speed — the very qualities that make an Elena indispensable under one set of conditions can become, under another, a quiet irritant. Not explicitly threatened. Not openly devalued. But subtly repositioned: a voice that carries institutional memory that no one currently in power wanted to accumulate, a presence that implicitly challenges the claim of the new direction to be entirely new. What Elena brought to the table may, in a period of radical organizational change, have become something harder to defend — not a threat surfaced, but a noise in the system.

In a period of more measured organizational change, these swings were manageable. The cycle turned, the organization rediscovered what it had lost, and Elena-type profiles were rehabilitated or replaced from a still-functioning pipeline. What the AI era has altered is both the speed of the swings and the depth of the pipeline. The cycles are faster — driven by a pace of technological change that makes transformation a permanent organizational state rather than a periodic disruption. And the pipeline that would replace the Elenas who are sidelined or lost is thinner than it has been at any point in the past thirty years.

The result is that what was previously a manageable rhythm of organizational self-correction is beginning to look more like a structural problem. Each swing costs a little more than the last. Each loss from the judgment pipeline is a little harder to replace. The organizational immune system — the capacity to recognize what it needs and reconstitute it — is functioning, but under increasing strain.

## What Organizations Get Wrong When They Try to Respond

At some level, most organizations sense this. The Russell Reynolds data shows that CEO confidence in C-suite succession has been declining steadily for years, despite — or perhaps because of — enormous investment in leadership development. The programs proliferate. The competency frameworks expand. The 360-degree reviews add new dimensions. And the gap between what organizations think they are building and what they actually produce continues to widen.

The specific mistake is worth identifying precisely, because it has a consistent structure across organizations.

The error begins with a confusion of categories: organizations treat the formation of judgment as if it were the transmission of knowledge. Knowledge can be documented, structured, packaged, and delivered through a program. Judgment cannot. Judgment is built through the mechanism described throughout this book — the repeated encounter with consequential complexity, with real stakes, with feedback that corrects and calibrates over time. No program can replicate this, because programs remove the two ingredients that formation requires: genuine stakes and genuine uncertainty.

When an organization runs a leadership development program, the participant knows it is a development program. The stakes are assessable, bounded, and ultimately performative rather than real. She is being evaluated, which means she will manage her performance in the exercise rather than navigating the problem as she would if the consequences were actually hers to carry. The feedback she receives is structured, sanitized, and delivered by someone whose job is to develop her rather than to hold her accountable for an outcome. None of this produces judgment. It produces something that resembles judgment — a facility with the language and frameworks of leadership — without the formation that makes those frameworks genuinely useful under pressure.

The second error follows from the first. Organizations confuse output quality with formation quality. When a person who has been directing AI-assisted tools produces excellent outputs — crisp presentations, sophisticated analyses, well-crafted strategic recommendations — the organization reads this as evidence of capability. In a narrow sense, it is. The outputs are excellent. What is not visible is whether the person who produced them would be capable of producing anything comparable if the AI were not available — or whether, more importantly, she would be capable of navigating the genuinely novel and ambiguous situations that AI cannot resolve on anyone's behalf.

The performance management system, built to measure individual contributions to measurable goals, has no instrument for this distinction. And because it has no instrument for it, it does not protect against the compounding formation loss that the AI era is driving. Organizations are granting the promotion, awarding the variable compensation, advancing the career — and not forming the judgment.

## The Asset That Cannot Be Inherited

There is a deeper economic truth about judgment-holders that organizations systematically fail to understand, and it goes beyond the measurement paradox.

Most valuable organizational assets depreciate at a manageable rate and can, in principle, be replaced. A building ages but can be maintained. A patent expires but can be renewed. A skilled employee retires, but the skills she held can, in principle, be recruited or developed in someone else. The asset is separable from the person who holds it.

Judgment, as this book has defined it, does not behave this way. It is not separable. The judgment that Elena holds — the accumulated, consequence-bearing, relationally embedded capacity to read what the environment is actually telling the organization — cannot be extracted and transferred. It cannot be documented, because it is not documentation that produced it. It cannot be trained in, because training is precisely what did not produce it. It was built through a specific trajectory of development that cannot be replicated at will.

This means that when an Elena retires or leaves, the organization does not lose an asset it can replace on the open market. It loses an asset it can only regenerate — through the same formation process that produced it — and only over the same time horizon that process requires. If the formation conditions no longer exist, the regeneration cannot happen. And this is the economic reality that most succession planning frameworks are not built to process: the asset being lost is not replaceable, in any practical sense, on any commercially relevant timeline.

The implication is structural. Organizations that understand this — that recognize judgment as a non-replicable, non-transferable asset whose only path of regeneration is through the deliberate maintenance of specific developmental conditions — will begin to treat the cultivation of judgment differently from the cultivation of any other capability. Not as a training investment. As a capital investment, with the long time horizons and patient accumulation that capital investment requires.

The organizations that do not understand this will continue to behave as though the asset can be replaced on demand — reaching backward for a retired leader when the pipeline fails, hiring expensive external talent when the internal succession comes up empty, and discovering each time that what they needed cannot be found on the open market at any price, because it was not produced by the open market. It was produced by conditions that were dismantled in the pursuit of efficiency, and that will take the better part of a generation to rebuild.

## The Question Underneath the Professional Question

There is a dimension to all of this that resists the economic frame entirely, and it surfaces in a specific kind of conversation — one that is becoming more common, and to which organizations have not yet found an adequate response.

It is the conversation with a mid-career professional who is confronting, in the most concrete terms, the automation of the work she spent a decade training for. Not in the abstract — not as a concern about future displacement — but in the present, as a daily experience of watching the tasks that constituted her professional identity being absorbed by systems that do them faster, more consistently, and without complaint.

On the surface, this is a professional question: what should she do? What skills should she develop? How should she position herself in a talent market that is restructuring around her? These are real questions and they deserve real answers. But underneath them — surfacing only when enough trust has been built, and usually only when enough time has passed for the professional implications to settle into something more personal — is a different question. Not what should she do. But what is she for?

This is not a question that competency frameworks can address. It is not a question that a leadership development program can resolve. It is the question that emerges when the work that organized a person's sense of

contribution and meaning is no longer the work that the market values —
and when the new form that her value is supposed to take has not yet been
adequately described or made available to her.

The organizations that are already navigating the judgment vacuum most
effectively are not the ones with the best reskilling programs or the most
sophisticated AI deployment strategies. They are the ones that have
maintained — deliberately or intuitively — the conditions under which
people encounter consequential complexity, are genuinely responsible for
outcomes, and are given enough space and enough time in the difficult
territory between not knowing and knowing to accumulate the formation
that gives work its meaning and gives the organization what it actually needs.

The human premium is not only an economic claim about scarcity and value.
It is an organizational claim about what it means to build something rather
than just operate it. And the organizations that will lead the next decade are
not the ones that recognize the economic logic first. They are the ones that
recognize what the economic logic is pointing at: that the thing which is
becoming scarce is not a skill, not a credential, and not a tool. It is a person
— formed by experience, shaped by consequence, capable of the particular
kind of judgment that neither systems nor programs can produce.

What that means for how work is structured, and for what work means to
the people doing it, is the subject of the chapter that follows.

## Notes

1. Russell Reynolds Associates, Leadership Confidence Index (H1 & H2
2025 Global Leadership Monitor, n = 732 global CEOs). Confidence in
C-suite succession scored 50.5 in 2025; the proportion of CEOs reporting a
successful C-suite succession strategy fell from 45 per cent in 2022 to 36 per
cent in 2023. Fewer than half of board directors believe their CEO succession
plans will succeed.

2. Jay B. Barney, 'Firm Resources and Sustained Competitive Advantage,' Journal of Management 17, no. 1 (1991): 99–120. Barney's VRIN framework — value, rarity, inimitability, and non-substitutability — remains the foundational test for durable strategic advantage in the resource-based view of the firm.

3. Russell Reynolds Associates, Transformational Leadership Study (2024). The report identifies 'crucible experiences' — high-stakes encounters with organizational complexity and change — as the primary differentiating factor in leaders who deliver successful transformation, ahead of any formal credential or competency assessment.

4. Greg Irving et al., 'International variations in primary care physician consultation time: a systematic review of 67 countries,' BMJ Open 7 (2017): e017902. The UK, with an average GP consultation duration of under ten minutes, ranks among the lowest in Europe. The Royal College of General Practitioners has called the ten-minute consultation unsustainable; a BMA survey found 92 per cent of GPs agreed.

5. The prohibition on recording internally developed intangible assets applies under both IFRS (IAS 38) and US GAAP. See Baruch Lev and Feng Gu, The End of Accounting and the Path Forward for Investors and Managers (Wiley, 2016) for the most comprehensive treatment of how accounting standards systematically obscure the value of knowledge and organizational capital.

6. Ocean Tomo, Intangible Asset Market Value Study (2020). The study tracks the shift in S&P 500 market value composition from 17 per cent intangible in 1975 to approximately 90 per cent intangible by 2020, representing a structural transformation in what drives organizational value.

# 9

# Identity at Work

*What work means when execution is automated, and why purpose and formation need to be redesigned together.*

There is a conversation that happens in every organization undergoing significant change, and it almost never surfaces in the room where the change is being designed. It happens in corridors, in one-on-ones that run long, in the pauses after a meeting has technically ended but nobody has yet moved toward the door. It happens when enough trust has accumulated for the professional question to give way to the personal one.

The professional question sounds like this: what should I do? What skills should I develop? How do I position myself for what comes next? These are real questions, and they deserve real answers. But they are also, in many cases, a socially acceptable container for a different question — one that the professional register makes difficult to ask directly.

The question underneath is simpler and harder: what am I for?

I have sat in enough of those conversations, across enough geographies and organizational layers, to recognize the pattern. The surface shifts — anxious in one city, philosophical in another, resigned somewhere else entirely —

but the underlying structure is consistent. What has changed is not the destination people are trying to reach. What has changed is the pace of the journey, and the discovery, somewhere along the way, that the map they were using no longer describes the terrain.

This chapter is about that discovery. It is not a chapter about career management or skills planning — those are real topics and they belong elsewhere. It is about something that sits above those topics: the relationship between work and identity, how that relationship has been quietly restructured by the forces this book has been tracing, and what needs to be redesigned — at the personal and organizational level — if work is to remain a place where people are formed rather than merely deployed.

## The Question That Organizations Cannot Answer

There is a specific dynamic that emerges when mid-career professionals confront the automation of the work that organized their professional identity. Not the work of junior colleagues — their own work. The analysis they spent years learning to produce. The modeling that constituted their expertise. The drafting that expressed their professional voice. When those tasks are absorbed by AI systems that do them faster, more consistently, and without apparent effort, something shifts in how a person understands their own contribution.

Research published in the Harvard Business Review in 2023 by Wharton's Stefano Puntoni and colleagues helps frame what is actually happening in that moment. Studying reactions to AI across multiple domains, they found that people who identify strongly with a particular skill or activity experience its automation not merely as a change in workflow but as a threat to identity itself. As Puntoni noted, people tend to view cognitive tasks as quite central to the sense of self — and when technology takes on tasks that are self-defining, the implicit question that surfaces is: who am I, if I am no longer the person who does this?[1]

That question has a specific character in the AI era that distinguishes it from earlier encounters with automation. Previous waves of automation removed tasks from the periphery of professional identity — the clerical, the administrative, the physically repetitive. The professional could absorb those changes because the tasks being automated were not the ones that defined professional worth. The sense of contribution remained anchored in the cognitive core: the analysis, the synthesis, the judgment that the automated system could not replicate.

AI removes that anchor. It absorbs the cognitive core. And it does so not in one specific domain, as earlier technologies did, but across all of them simultaneously. The GPS removed one form of navigational competence. AI challenges drafting and analysis and strategic framing and communication — all at once, in every direction, with a scope and speed that earlier technological transitions did not approach.

The result is a kind of professional disorientation that organizations are not well-equipped to address, because it does not resolve through the mechanisms organizations typically reach for. Training programs address skill gaps. Competency frameworks address performance gaps. Neither addresses the question of what work means when the tasks that made it meaningful have been absorbed by a system that has no stake in the outcome.

## What Formation Feels Like from the Inside

Most of this book has treated formation as something organizations need — the mechanism through which judgment is built and transmitted across generations. That framing is accurate, and the organizational stakes are real. But formation is also something the person experiences. And if we are to understand why its erosion matters beyond the organizational consequences — why it registers as a loss rather than merely a structural change — we need to understand what it feels like to be in the middle of it.

Mihaly Csikszentmihalyi's research on optimal experience offers a useful entry point. Across decades of empirical work, Csikszentmihalyi found that the conditions that produce the deepest engagement and satisfaction in human activity are not ease or comfort — they are challenge matched to skill, with clear feedback and genuine stakes.[2] The psychological state he called flow — a condition of absorbed, purposeful engagement in which self-consciousness recedes and time distorts — occurs precisely when the task is demanding enough to require full deployment of capability, and when the outcome is genuinely uncertain.

The relevance to formation is direct. What the apprenticeship chain produced, at its best, was not a sequence of tasks to be completed — it was a sequence of encounters with consequential complexity, each one demanding enough to push the person beyond their current capability, each one producing feedback that calibrated judgment and built the kind of embodied confidence that only comes from having navigated difficulty and survived it. The junior analyst who stayed late with a CFO working through a pricing model did not merely learn to build pricing models. She learned what it felt like to hold real stakes, to be uncertain under pressure, and to arrive at a judgment that the organization would actually act on. That experience — repeated, accumulated, progressively deepened — is what formation produces. And Csikszentmihalyi's research suggests why it is also, experientially, what makes work feel meaningful: not the completion of routine tasks, but the encounter with difficulty that stretches capability and produces growth.

Conversely, the research also illuminates what is lost when that encounter disappears. A workforce whose primary mode is operating AI-assisted tools — directing rather than doing, reviewing rather than producing — is a workforce that has been systematically removed from the conditions that produce both formation and engagement. The challenge-skill balance that Csikszentmihalyi identified as the precondition for deep engagement requires that the skill be genuinely deployed and tested under real conditions.

When the system does the work, the skill atrophies, and the engagement that depends on its deployment fades with it. What remains is something closer to what Csikszentmihalyi called apathy: the state that occurs when both challenge and skill are low, and where neither the anxiety of real difficulty nor the satisfaction of genuine competence is available.

Science fiction has long sensed this danger even when organizations have not. The genre's most persistent image of a technologically stratified society is not a story of revolt or collapse — it is a story of quiet bifurcation. On one side, the small circle of elders who hold genuine authority: people whose accumulated formation makes them capable of reading the environment, weighing consequences, and making judgments that the system cannot make for them. On the other side, a much larger population defined by its relationship to routine: interchangeable, their attention trained on data streams, performing the monitoring and operating functions that the automated world requires. The elders are few. The operators are many. And the most unsettling element of those images is not the hierarchy — it is the absence of a path between the two. The operators do not become elders. The formation conditions that would make that journey possible have long since disappeared. What the fiction imagines as dystopia, the current trajectory of organizational design is beginning to produce as an unremarkable operational outcome.

This is not a theoretical projection. It is already visible in the pattern that the opening of this chapter described: the professional who moves from initial enthusiasm at AI-enhanced outputs to a quieter, more persistent discomfort — not with the quality of the output, but with the absence of the encounter that used to make producing it feel like something.

# The Honest Admission

There is a dimension to this that I want to be direct about, because it describes something I recognize in myself as much as in the people I have sat across from in those corridor conversations.

When AI absorbs significant portions of what you used to produce, the experience has two sides. The first is an immediate and genuine appreciation: the output is better. The analysis is more thorough, the narrative more polished, the communication more precisely calibrated than what you could have produced alone. That appreciation is real, and it lasts for a moment.

The second is less comfortable. It is a quiet sense of not being entirely honest with yourself — because that better quality was not generated by you. You directed it. You shaped it. You reviewed and adjusted it. But you did not produce it in the way that used to feel like production. The thing that arrived in the world did not come through you in the way that earlier things did.

I am aware that this feeling has historical echoes. People said something similar about spreadsheets, about word processors, about GPS navigation. Each new tool produced a version of the same anxiety — that the competence being augmented was also, in some sense, being replaced. And in each case, the anxiety eventually resolved as the tool was integrated into a new sense of professional identity that accommodated it.

But there is a structural difference with AI that makes those earlier analogies only partially transferable. Earlier tools augmented specific, bounded domains of capability. The spreadsheet changed financial modeling; it did not change how you read a room, managed a relationship, or made a judgment call under pressure. AI augments everything — all at once, in all directions — including the cognitive tasks that used to be the residual sanctuary of human contribution after the administrative and physical layers had been automated. The scope is different. The speed is different. And the consequence is that the process of identity reconstruction that resolved earlier waves of technological change has less time and less anchoring ground to work with.

The management scholar Amy Wrzesniewski has spent decades studying what she calls work orientation — the distinction between people who experience their work as a job, a career, or a calling. Her research finds that roughly a third of workers fall into each category, and that the calling orientation — where work is experienced as integral to identity and as a form of contribution that extends beyond personal advancement — is associated with the deepest engagement and the highest levels of both personal satisfaction and organizational value-creation.[3] What the AI era threatens, specifically, is the conditions under which calling orientation can be sustained. When the tasks through which a person enacts their calling are absorbed by a system that has no calling, the calling itself becomes harder to locate. The question — what am I for? — is, in Wrzesniewski's terms, the question of where the calling now lives when the tasks that expressed it have moved elsewhere.

## The Speed Problem

The adaptation that earlier technological transitions eventually produced did not happen quickly. It happened over years and decades, as organizations and individuals worked out new configurations of human and machine contribution — new definitions of what professional expertise meant in a world where certain tasks had been automated. The generation that absorbed the spreadsheet had time to reconstruct a sense of professional identity around the remaining cognitive complexity. The generation that absorbed word processing had time to locate its contribution in the judgment and creativity that the processing layer could not replicate.

What the AI era has altered is not the direction of that reconstruction — it is the time available to complete it. And it has altered something else: the scope of what remains after the automation has occurred.

William Bridges, whose work on organizational transition has been influential for four decades, made a distinction that is useful here. Change, he argued, is the external event — the structural shift, the technological implementation, the reorganization. Transition is the internal process through which people come to terms with the change and reconstitute a functional sense of identity and purpose on the other side of it.[4] What organizations consistently underestimate is the duration and depth of transition — the period he called the Neutral Zone, in which the old identity is no longer operative but the new one has not yet formed. That period is not empty. It is the space in which the psychological work of reconstruction actually happens. And it requires time.

The AI era is compressing the time available for that transition while simultaneously expanding its scope. The people who sat across from me in those corridor conversations were not primarily anxious about job loss — though that anxiety was often present at the surface. They were navigating something deeper: the discovery that the psychological reconstruction they had expected to have time to complete was being demanded faster than the formation process that makes reconstruction possible. They were being asked to arrive at a new sense of purpose before they had fully understood what had been lost.

This compression is not just a personal inconvenience. It has organizational consequences that compound the formation problem described throughout this book. A workforce in prolonged transition — uncertain about what its contribution means, unable to locate its identity in the tasks that used to define it, not yet having arrived at the new sense of purpose that would anchor engagement — is a workforce that cannot form the next generation of judgment holders. Formation requires presence, not just proximity. It requires people who are grounded enough in their own sense of contribution to transmit the thing that makes their contribution valuable. An organization full of people navigating their own identity reconstruction cannot simultaneously be an organization that builds judgment in others.

# The Operator Problem

There is a specific risk that deserves naming directly, because it represents the most probable failure mode if the identity question is left unaddressed.

When execution is automated and the human role is defined primarily as operating the automated system — directing, reviewing, adjusting, deploying — the human in that role faces a specific psychological condition that is different from mere disengagement. It is the condition of having genuine capability and genuine intelligence available, but no natural context in which to deploy them. The challenge-skill balance that Csikszentmihalyi identified as the precondition for engagement is not merely disrupted — it is eliminated. The system absorbs the challenge. The human provides the instruction.

This is not a future projection. I have watched it happen in the organizations I have worked with. The junior professional who directs an AI tool to produce analysis that she would previously have built herself does not become less intelligent in the process. Her analytical capability does not disappear. But it does not develop either — because the encounter with difficulty that development requires has been removed from her daily experience. And over time, something more insidious occurs: she begins to doubt whether the capability was hers to begin with. The AI-assisted output is excellent. The unassisted output, on the rare occasions it is required, is less so. The gap between the two becomes, gradually, a form of self-distrust.

Research on worker autonomy and AI-mediated decision-making confirms the mechanism. A 2025 study published in the journal Computers in Human Behavior found that as AI systems increasingly assume higher-level decision-making responsibilities once reserved for humans, the consequences include not just reduced skill development but diminished perception of the meaningfulness of the task itself — a finding consistent with self-determination theory's prediction that perceived competence and autonomy are foundational to intrinsic motivation.[5]

The practical consequence for organizations is a workforce that is, in the precise sense of the word, dormant. Not incompetent — dormant. The capability is present but not activated; the intelligence is available but not deployed in the conditions that would develop it. And dormancy compounds over time, as the gap between what the AI-assisted professional can produce and what she could produce without the system widens. The judgment vacuum that this book has been tracing is not only a pipeline problem — an absence of formed judgment in the leadership succession. It is also, increasingly, a present-tense problem: a workforce with genuine potential that is being systematically prevented from developing it by the very tools that are making its outputs look excellent.

There is a harder question embedded in this analysis, and it is worth acknowledging honestly: what if dormancy is not an unintended consequence but a rational one? The economic logic of automation points in a clear direction. AI capability is cheaper than human capability, more consistent, and available at scale. A workforce that has been reduced to an operating role — directing systems, reviewing outputs, managing exceptions — requires less investment in development, less tolerance for the inefficiency that formation demands, and generates less of the organizational friction that comes with people who hold strong independent judgment. From a short-term efficiency standpoint, a dormant workforce is a contained one. Leadership that maximizes near-term returns has a rational, if uncomfortable, incentive to accept dormancy as the price of automation — and to regard the judgment vacuum not as a crisis to be addressed but as a transitional state on the way to a leaner model. This book does not accept that conclusion. But it does not pretend the logic is absent. Organizations that choose the path of deliberate formation will be choosing something that requires more investment, more patience, and more willingness to hold complexity than the optimized alternative. The argument for that choice is not that it is easier. It is that the organizations which make it will be the ones still capable of genuine strategic action in a decade's time — and that the ones which do not will discover, too late, that they optimized away the very capability that made optimization worth pursuing.

# Where Identity Can Be Re-Anchored

The question that emerges from all of this is not whether professional identity needs to be reconstructed — it clearly does. The question is what it can be anchored to when the task layer has been substantially automated.

I want to be precise about what this is not. It is not a call to resist or circumvent AI — that would be both futile and self-defeating. The efficiency and quality gains are real, and an organization that chose to forgo them for the sake of preserving a particular configuration of human contribution would be choosing competitive disadvantage without developmental benefit. Nor is it a call to locate human identity in the tasks that AI cannot yet perform — because that is a moving frontier that will not hold, and a professional identity anchored to AI's current limitations is an identity with a diminishing foundation.

What it is, instead, is a claim about what endures — and about what organizations need to deliberately create the conditions for.

Formation, as this book has defined it, is the process through which a person develops the capacity to hold consequential complexity: to read situations that have not been read before, to make judgments in conditions of genuine uncertainty, to carry the weight of decisions whose outcomes are genuinely theirs to own. That process does not happen through task execution alone — but it does require real stakes, real difficulty, and real feedback. What needs to be redesigned is not the human contribution but the conditions under which human contribution develops. Not what people produce, but what they encounter in the process of producing it.

This means that the organizations that will navigate the AI era most effectively are not the ones that automate most aggressively and then try to address the human consequences as a secondary problem. They are the ones that are deliberate about maintaining — or creating, where they do not currently exist — the developmental conditions that formation requires. They keep people in contact with consequential complexity. They ensure that AI augmentation does not remove the encounter with difficulty that makes augmentation meaningful. They define professional contribution not by output quality alone but by the judgment that the person is developing in the process of directing and applying the system.

At the personal level, this requires a shift in how professionals locate their own identity. Not in the task — which is increasingly automated. Not in the output — which is increasingly excellent regardless of the human's developmental state. But in the judgment: the specific, accumulated, contextually embedded capacity to determine what the output means, what it requires, what its consequences are, and what to do with it. That is the contribution that neither the system nor the program can replicate. It is also, increasingly, the contribution that the organization most needs — and the one that is hardest to sustain if the conditions that produce it are systematically removed.

## Purpose as the New Organizing Principle

The conversation that this chapter began with — the one in the corridor, after the meeting, when the professional question gives way to the personal one — does not typically resolve through a skills planning discussion. It resolves, when it resolves, through an encounter with purpose: a clarified understanding of what the person's contribution is actually for, beyond the task that used to express it.

That is not a therapeutic observation. It is an organizational one. Purpose is not a soft complement to the serious business of performance management — it is, in conditions of rapid automation, the primary mechanism through which professional identity can remain stable enough to support formation. A professional who understands clearly why their judgment matters, what specifically it contributes that the AI system cannot, and in what conditions their accumulated formation is the thing that makes the organization capable of navigating complexity — that professional has an identity anchor that is durable in a way that task-based identity is not.

I have experienced this directly, on both sides of the conversation. There were a handful of leaders, across the course of my own career, who took the time to place my work in its larger context — who explained not just what I was being asked to produce, but where it would travel, whose decisions it would shape, and what would have been impossible without it. Those conversations were, in retrospect, disproportionately important. Not because they added tasks or changed deliverables. Because they changed the meaning of the work that was already there. The analysis I was doing before that conversation was technically identical to the analysis I did after it. But after it, the work was connected to something. The engagement that followed was not manufactured or incentivised — it was the natural consequence of understanding that the contribution was real and that it mattered beyond the immediate transaction.

I observed the same dynamic with junior teams throughout my career. When I sat with a group and explained what their work was actually for — who used it, how it connected to decisions being made elsewhere in the organization, what would have been worse without it — the energy in the room changed. Not because the work changed. Because the people doing it understood, perhaps for the first time, that they were not just executing tasks but participating in something that extended beyond their immediate line of sight. That understanding is not complicated to produce. It requires a leader willing to invest fifteen minutes in explanation rather than instruction. But it is also, in most organizations, systematically absent — crowded out by the pressure for immediate output that makes the connective conversation feel like a luxury rather than the foundational act of formation it actually is.

The organizations that are already navigating this most effectively have not resolved it through new frameworks or refreshed competency models. They have maintained — sometimes deliberately, sometimes intuitively — a clarity about what they are asking their people to be. Not operators. Not reviewers. Not prompt engineers. Judgment holders: people who are in the process of developing the formation that makes the organization capable of acting intelligently in conditions that the system cannot resolve. That definition of contribution gives the corridor conversation somewhere to land. It gives the professional a response to the question — what am I for? — that is not dependent on the continuity of any specific task.

It also, as the final section of this book will argue, requires a specific kind of organizational architecture to sustain. The redesign of work for the judgment era is not primarily a technology deployment question. It is a formation question — and answering it requires the kind of leadership, the kind of deliberate friction, and the kind of organizational design that the next three chapters will describe.

*"The question is not whether AI will change what work requires. It already has. The question is whether organizations will redesign work in a way that continues to produce the thing that AI cannot — the formed human judgment that emerges from genuine encounter with consequence. That redesign begins with a willingness to take seriously the question that is already being asked in corridors everywhere: not what should I do, but what am I for."*

## Notes

1. Gizem Yalcin and Stefano Puntoni, 'How AI Affects Our Sense of Self,' Harvard Business Review (September–October 2023). The research documents how automation of identity-central tasks produces identity threat responses distinct from those triggered by automation of peripheral tasks — a finding with direct implications for professional identity in knowledge work.

2. Mihaly Csikszentmihalyi, Flow: The Psychology of Optimal Experience (Harper & Row, 1990). The conditions Csikszentmihalyi identifies for flow

— challenge-skill balance, clear goals, immediate feedback, genuine stakes — map directly onto the conditions that the apprenticeship chain historically provided, and that systematic automation has systematically removed.

3. Amy Wrzesniewski, Clark McCauley, Paul Rozin, and Barry Schwartz, 'Jobs, Careers, and Callings: People's Relations to Their Work,' Journal of Research in Personality 31, no. 1 (1997): 21–33. Wrzesniewski's calling orientation — where work is integral to identity and experienced as socially purposeful — is associated with the highest levels of both personal satisfaction and organisational contribution. Its erosion under conditions of extensive automation has implications that extend well beyond individual wellbeing.

4. William Bridges, Transitions: Making Sense of Life's Changes (Addison-Wesley, 1980; revised edition, Da Capo Press, 2004). Bridges's distinction between change (the external event) and transition (the internal psycho-logical process of reconstitution) is foundational to understanding why organizations consistently underestimate the human cost of technological transformation. The Neutral Zone — the period between the old identity and the new — is not empty time; it is where the psychological work of reconstruction actually occurs, and it cannot be compressed without cost.

5. See research summarized in 'Safeguarding Worker Psychosocial Well-being in the Age of AI: The Critical Role of Decision Control,' Computers in Human Behavior (2025), drawing on self-determination theory (Deci and Ryan) to demonstrate that AI-mediated reduction of decision authority pro-duces measurable decreases in perceived task meaningfulness and intrinsic motivation — consequences that are independent of, and compound, the formation losses described throughout this book.

# 10

# The New Leader's Job



*Moment IV — The Design Imperative*

*What leadership actually looks like when your primary responsibility is not efficiency but human formation and organizational adaptability.*

There is a specific kind of meeting that stays with you long after it ends — not because of what was decided, but because of how the room felt. Everyone present knew what they thought. Everyone had an opinion. But nobody was waiting for permission to say it. The conversation moved, circled back, sharpened, and arrived somewhere that nobody had anticipated at the start. And when it was over, you did not feel depleted by the process. You felt enlarged by it.

Those rooms are rarer than they should be. Most meetings in most organizations do not feel like that. They feel like briefings — information flowing in one direction, questions cautiously phrased, conclusions pre-agreed. People arrive knowing broadly what will be said and leave broadly confirmed in what they already believed. Nobody is challenged. Nobody grows. Nobody, if we are honest, is really present.

The difference between those two kinds of rooms is not accidental. It is not a matter of personality or luck or culture in some vague, unfalsifiable sense. It is a direct consequence of what the leader in that room believes their job to be.

For most of the automation era, we have operated with a particular model of what leadership means. The leader is the accountability holder. The leader's job is to define objectives, allocate resources, remove obstacles, and ensure delivery. Everything else — the development of people, the cultivation of judgment, the creation of conditions for thinking — is important, yes, but secondary. It happens after the real work is done, if it happens at all.

This model was adequate, even well-suited, for an era in which the primary challenge of organizations was execution. When the environment was stable enough to be planned against, when tasks could be decomposed and delegated with confidence, when the systems were the point — efficiency-first leadership made sense. It rewarded the right things and produced the right outcomes.

But we are not in that era anymore. And the leaders who understand this — who have already shifted their model of the job, even if they have not yet found the language for it — are building something qualitatively different from the organizations around them. They are not just better-run. They are better at becoming.

## Two Leaders, One Organization

Imagine two leaders who each take charge of the same large professional organization at different points in its history. The organization is successful by conventional measures: it has strong revenue, a well-known name, and a workforce of tens of thousands of people. The incoming leader in each case inherits something that works.

The first leader does something that is difficult to classify in the conventional vocabulary of management. They do not redesign the operating model. They do not restructure the hierarchy. What they do is subtler and, in the long run, far more consequential: they change what gets rewarded. Ideas that once had to travel upward through layers of approval are now welcomed where they originate. Capabilities with no obvious short-term efficiency return — ways of working that are about creativity and curiosity and cross-disciplinary thinking — are invested in. Mistakes made in the service of learning do not end careers. The signal sent, repeatedly and consistently, is that this organization is a knowledge machine, and knowledge machines run on the intellectual engagement of the people inside them.

Something happens as a result that conventional metrics struggle to capture. The organization begins to function as though it is considerably larger than it actually is. Not because headcount has grown, but because discretionary energy has been unlocked — the effort that goes beyond the contract, the initiative that goes beyond the instruction, the kind of contribution that people only make when they feel that what they are building genuinely belongs to them. People are not doing what they are told. They are doing what they believe in. That distinction, multiplied across thousands of individuals, is the difference between an organization that performs and one that compounds.

The second leader brings a different theory. Authority migrates back toward the center. Directions become clearer, and more final. People who have spent years developing deep knowledge of clients, markets, and organizational context — knowledge that exists nowhere else in the institution — find that this knowledge is no longer what is wanted from them. What is wanted is execution. The organization experiences a specific kind of disorientation: not the productive uncertainty that comes from genuine complexity, but the demoralizing confusion of people who have been told to run and are suddenly being asked to walk in formation.

Financially, the organization in this period does not collapse. Revenues hold.

By the measures that appear in quarterly reports, performance continues. And that is precisely the insidious quality of what is happening. The damage does not show up in the numbers immediately, because the numbers measure outputs, and outputs are still being delivered — by people drawing down on reserves of institutional knowledge, contextual judgment, and relational capital that were built under different conditions and are not being replenished. The pipeline is still flowing. What is not visible yet is that the source is quietly running dry.

What changes first is not output but formation. The conditions under which judgment develops begin to erode. The organization becomes more reliable in the short run and less capable of generating the future. In the language of this book: it gets better at executing what it already knows and progressively less able to respond well to what it does not yet know. The judgment vacuum widens.

I am not describing a moral failure on the part of the second leader. Both leaders in this composite portrait were making choices they believed were rational and right. What I am pointing at is something structural: two different theories of what the leader's job is, operating inside the same institution, producing environments with fundamentally different consequences for the human development that is the invisible substrate of long-term performance.

This is not a rare or unusual dynamic. Variations of it play out in organizations of every size, in every sector, with regularity. The names and industries change. The mechanism does not.

## What the Job Actually Is

Ronald Heifetz of Harvard's Kennedy School spent decades distinguishing between what he called technical problems and adaptive challenges. Technical problems — even very complex ones — can be solved by expertise and good management. Someone with the right knowledge can diagnose the issue and apply the solution. Adaptive challenges are different. They require changes in people's values, beliefs, habits, and priorities. They cannot be solved by experts acting on others. The people who have the problem are the people who must generate the solution.

Heifetz's central argument, developed across his body of work culminating in The Practice of Adaptive Leadership with Alexander Grashow and Marty Linsky, is that the central failure of leadership is to treat adaptive challenges as though they were technical problems. To apply expertise where what is needed is learning. To provide direction where what is needed is engagement. To resolve the tension prematurely, before the people in the system have done the work of genuinely changing.[1]

The judgment vacuum is an adaptive challenge. It cannot be solved by a training program, however well-designed. It cannot be solved by a mentoring scheme, however thoughtfully matched. It cannot be solved by any technical intervention that leaves the underlying conditions — the conditions under which judgment forms — unchanged. It requires leaders who understand that their primary responsibility is to design and maintain the environment in which adaptive capacity develops.

This is a different job description than the one most leaders have been given. It requires letting go of something that many leaders find deeply uncomfortable: the certainty of the expert. The leader who is accountable for formation is not the person with the right answer. They are the person who creates the conditions in which right answers can emerge — from the people who are closest to the problem, in the moment when the problem requires judgment that no procedure can anticipate.

Robert Greenleaf named this inversion more than fifty years ago, in his foundational 1970 essay The Servant as Leader. His formulation was deliberately challenging: the servant-leader, he argued, is servant first. Not in the sense of subservience, but in the sense of priority — their primary orientation is toward the growth and development of those they lead. The best test of servant leadership, Greenleaf wrote, is whether those being served grow as persons: whether they become healthier, wiser, freer, more autonomous, and more capable themselves of leadership.[2]

This was considered radical when Greenleaf wrote it. In the context of the judgment vacuum, it has become practical necessity.

## The Identity Shift

Moving from efficiency-first to formation-first leadership is not, at its core, a skills problem. Leaders who make this shift successfully are not people who have attended the right training courses. They are people who have genuinely revised their understanding of what their role is for.

That revision is much harder than it sounds, because the efficiency-first model is not just a management philosophy. It is an identity. Leaders who have built careers around accountability for results — who define themselves through the clarity of their objectives, the sharpness of their priorities, and the discipline of their execution — experience the shift to formation-first leadership as a genuine loss. The loss of certainty. The loss of control. The loss of the clean, measurable satisfaction of a problem solved.

I have seen this play out in a specific way in the leaders I have worked with. The ones who struggle most with the shift are precisely the ones who are most skilled at the old model. Their competence has become their cage. They are excellent at moving things forward, at driving to clarity, at getting things done. And so every room they enter becomes a room in which things get moved forward, driven to clarity, and gotten done — even when what the room actually needed was for people to sit with difficulty for a little longer.

The micromanager — and I use the term descriptively, not pejoratively — is a leader who has discovered that they can reduce uncertainty by expanding their presence in every decision. They feel safe when they control the output. And in an efficiency-first world, this approach is often rewarded, because it does reduce variance. But it also eliminates the conditions under which the people around them can develop judgment. When every decision is reviewed, every direction is pre-approved, and every error is caught before it can teach anything, the organization becomes technically reliable and developmentally inert.

The contrasting model is the leader who invests fifteen minutes in explaining the broader context of why a task matters before asking someone to do it. Who is willing to tolerate the slightly longer timeline that comes with allowing someone to find their own path to the right answer, rather than pointing them directly at it. Who distinguishes — and this distinction is operationally important — between objectives and consequences.

Consider cost reduction as an example. A leader who sets cost reduction as an objective will get cost reduction. But the consequences of that framing are often higher than the savings it generates: exhausted teams, institutional knowledge lost, motivation drained, and a single improvement rather than a durable capability. A leader who positions cost reduction as a consequence — of finding efficiencies, of rethinking processes, of enabling the people closest to the work to surface what they know — will also get cost reduction, usually at similar scale. But they will also get something more durable: a team that is developing the capacity to think about efficiency structurally, rather than executing against a target. And the next time the challenge comes, they will not be starting from scratch.

This is not idealism. It is a different theory of compounding. Efficiency-first leaders capture the value of the present. Formation-first leaders compound the capacity of the future.

# What It Looks Like on a Tuesday Afternoon

Principles without practice are philosophy. So let me describe what the formation-first leadership model actually looks like in operational terms — not in strategic documents or annual reviews, but in the texture of ordinary working days.

The most reliable indicator I have found is what a leader does with ambiguity. When a situation arises that does not fit the existing playbook — a client relationship that is deteriorating for reasons that are not yet clear, a market shift that the numbers are not yet capturing, a team dynamic that is producing outputs but killing something harder to measure — the efficiency-first leader moves immediately to resolution. They call a meeting, define the problem, assign an owner, and set a deadline. The discomfort of unresolved ambiguity is rapidly eliminated.

The formation-first leader does something different. They bring people into the ambiguity rather than protecting them from it. They ask questions that they do not already have the answer to. They create, in Amy Edmondson of Harvard Business School's terms, psychological safety — a climate in which people feel it is safe to speak up, to share incomplete thinking, to name what they are seeing even before they know what it means.[3] Not because comfort is the goal, but because the productive friction of genuine uncertainty is precisely the condition in which judgment forms.

This looks, from the outside, like a more relaxed organization. And in one sense it is: there is less of the anxious, performative urgency that characterizes environments where everyone is afraid of the wrong answer. But it is not a comfortable organization in any deep sense. It is an organization that is doing something harder than executing: it is continuously becoming.

Practically, this shows up in how leaders structure their time. The formation-first leader spends a disproportionate amount of their calendar in conversations that have no immediate deliverable — not briefings, but genuine exchanges in which they are learning something they did not know, and the person they are talking to is being asked to think at the edge of what they already understand. They are visible in the organization not primarily through formal review processes but through the quality of their presence in informal moments: the question asked after a presentation that takes it somewhere the presenter had not anticipated, the observation shared in a corridor that reframes a problem someone has been stuck on for weeks.

They also do something that sounds simple but is, in practice, deeply counter intuitive for leaders who have been formed by the efficiency model: they allow failure to teach. Not catastrophic failure — the goal is not recklessness. But the smaller, recoverable errors from which learning can be extracted are not suppressed. They are named, examined, and sometimes even celebrated. Because an organization that has eliminated the conditions for failure has also eliminated the conditions for growth.

## The Paradox of the Formed

There is a genuine paradox at the heart of this chapter, and it deserves to be faced directly rather than reasoned away.

The leaders who are best positioned to redesign for formation are the ones who carry the most judgment. They are the survivors of the apprenticeship chain described in Chapter 1 — people who were shaped by friction, by proximity to consequence, by years of absorbing context that was never formally transmitted but was always implicitly present. They understand, in their bones, what it means to develop as a professional over time.

But the very fact that their formation was accidental — that it happened to them rather than being designed for them — can make it paradoxically difficult to see what needs to be designed. People who acquired something through a process they did not consciously manage often find it hard to deconstruct that process. They know what they know, but they cannot always explain the conditions that produced the knowing.

And there is a second layer to this paradox. The leaders who most successfully formed judgment under the old system were often the ones who were most comfortable in uncertain, friction-filled, unstructured environments. They thrived on ambiguity because ambiguity was where the real work happened. But this comfort with uncertainty is not evenly distributed. The leaders who struggled in those environments — who sought more structure, more clarity, more direction — were not failing. They were exhibiting a human response to discomfort. And some of those leaders, responding rationally to the discomfort they experienced, became the micromanagers and the centralizers. They built the controlled environments that eliminated the very friction that had formed them.

I think the resolution to this paradox is not a matter of experience — of having been formed in one way versus another. It is a matter of how you process the formation journey, and how you relate to uncertainty.

The leaders who are capable of the shift are not necessarily those who have the most experience. They are those who have developed what might be called a generative relationship with not-knowing. They have learned — sometimes through hard experience, sometimes through conscious reflection — that the output of their organization is not the highest expression of their capability. The growth of the people around them is. These are the leaders who delegate not because they have too much to do, but because they see that the output is genuinely better when people are given the space to find their own path to it.

They expand rather than restrict. And in doing so, they create the conditions for something that efficiency-first leadership, by its very nature, cannot produce: an organization that gets better at getting better.

# A Note on What This Is Not

It is worth pausing to name a version of this argument that I am not making, because it is the version most likely to provoke the kind of resistance I described earlier — the polite nod, the private skepticism, the post-meeting corridor conversation that begins with 'that's all very well, but…'.

Formation-first leadership is not a rejection of accountability. It is a deepening of it. The leader who is accountable only for this quarter's results is accountable for a narrow slice of what actually matters. The leader who is accountable for the judgment capacity of their organization — for whether the people they are developing will still be capable of making good decisions in three years, when the current generation of senior leaders is no longer there to catch the errors — is accountable for something far harder to measure and far more consequential.

It is also not a rejection of efficiency. The genuine benefits of AI — the speed, the scale, the analytical horsepower that has been legitimately and valuably deployed across organizations over the past decade — are real, and surrendering them would be foolish. The argument of this book has never been that automation was a mistake. The argument is that the loss of formation was an unintended consequence that we can now, with enough awareness and enough design intention, begin to address. Efficiency and formation are not in opposition. They have simply been managed as though they were, for long enough that their relationship has been forgotten.

The discrepancy that I observe most often in conversations about formation-first leadership — and I use discrepancy deliberately, because resistance implies a rigidity that most of these conversations do not have — is not a disagreement with the diagnosis. Most leaders who have been in their organizations long enough can see the hollowing. The discrepancy is about the mechanism: what does it actually mean to redesign for formation, inside the constraints of an organization that still has quarterly targets and board expectations and a competitive environment that does not pause while the redesign takes effect?

That question is a real one. The next two chapters address it directly. But the prerequisite for answering it is already in place by the time a leader has genuinely accepted the reframing of their job. Because once you understand that your primary responsibility is not efficiency but formation — that your most important output is not this year's delivery but the judgment capacity of the organization you are leaving to whoever comes next — the practical questions become navigable. They are still hard. But they are the right questions.

# The Formation-First Leader in an AI-Augmented World

There is one final dimension to the new leader's job that deserves direct attention, because it is both the most consequential and the most misunderstood aspect of leading in the current moment.

AI is not going to go away. It is not going to slow down. And the leaders who respond to the arguments in this book by attempting to simply reduce their organization's AI dependency — to reintroduce friction by removing the tools that eliminated it — will fail, for the same reason that the firms that refused to adopt ERP systems in the 1990s eventually failed: not because the technology was perfect, but because the competitive environment would not wait for their reservations.

The goal, therefore, is not less AI. It is better AI deployment — designed by leaders who understand that the question is not what AI can do, but what it should do, and what should remain irreducibly human.

The emerging research on human-AI collaboration is beginning to clarify what this looks like in practice. The sustainable competitive advantage of the next decade will not come from wholesale automation — the deployment of

AI wherever it can technically replace human effort — but from what might be called augmented intelligence: the deliberate design of human-AI systems that combine the analytical horsepower of machines with the contextual judgment, ethical navigation, and relational intelligence of people who have been genuinely developed.[4] Neither humans nor AI alone. Both, in designed collaboration, doing what each does best.

The formation-first leader's role in this ecosystem is specific and important. It is to ask, continuously and concretely, which elements of the organization's work are being appropriately augmented — made better, faster, more accurate by AI — and which are being inappropriately automated: replaced in ways that eliminate the productive friction through which human judgment forms. The goal is not to resist the former. It is to protect the latter.

This requires a kind of discrimination that only humans can exercise — and only humans who have themselves developed judgment. The leader who has never built a pricing model by hand cannot intuitively sense when the AI's pricing model has quietly encoded an assumption that the market has moved past. The leader who has never navigated a difficult client relationship without a decision-support system cannot recognize the moment when the system's recommendation is technically correct but humanly wrong. The formation-first leader is not protecting inefficiency. They are protecting the developmental conditions from which the human judgment that AI cannot replace is produced.

What this means, practically, is that the formation-first leader in an AI-augmented organization is making a specific set of decisions that their efficiency-first counterpart is not making. They are deciding which tasks should remain human-led, not because AI cannot do them, but because doing them is how people learn. They are designing workflows in which AI handles the pattern-matching and humans engage with the anomalies — the situations that fall outside the pattern, where the stakes of getting it wrong are high and the machine's confidence is unreliable. They are deliberately creating the moments of productive difficulty that the efficiency-first deployment of AI systematically eliminates.

And they are doing something subtler still: they are ensuring that when people in their organization work with AI tools, they understand what the AI is doing well enough to challenge it. Not to reject it reflexively, but to engage with its outputs as a skilled collaborator engages with any input — accepting what is sound, questioning what is uncertain, and overriding what is wrong. The organization whose people can do this well is not just more resilient than the one whose people cannot. It is developing a kind of institutional intelligence that no pure automation strategy can replicate.

This is the optimal ecosystem that the formation-first leader is building: not an organization that uses AI less, but one that uses it with judgment. Where the deployment of AI is itself a design decision — made by people who understand what is being preserved and what is being replaced. Where the time that AI genuinely frees up is reinvested deliberately into the formation activities that automation has otherwise been quietly eliminating for thirty years.

The leader who builds that ecosystem is doing something historically unusual: designing an organization that gets smarter as it gets more efficient, rather than despite it. That is the new leader's job. And it is, without question, harder than the old one.

## Notes

[1]Ronald A. Heifetz, Alexander Grashow, and Marty Linsky, The Practice of Adaptive Leadership: Tools and Tactics for Changing Your Organization and the World (Boston: Harvard Business Press, 2009). Heifetz's earlier foun-

dational work on the distinction between technical problems and adaptive challenges appeared in Leadership Without Easy Answers (Cambridge, MA: Harvard University Press, 1994).

[2]Robert K. Greenleaf, The Servant as Leader (Cambridge, MA: Center for Applied Studies, 1970). Greenleaf's formulation of the test of servant leadership — whether those being served grow as persons — remains one of the most precise and demanding definitions of the leader's developmental responsibility in the literature.

[3]Amy C. Edmondson, The Fearless Organization: Creating Psychological Safety in the Workplace for Learning, Innovation, and Growth (Hoboken, NJ: John Wiley & Sons, 2018). Edmondson defines psychological safety as a climate in which people feel comfortable expressing and being themselves — the foundation for the kind of learning that judgment formation requires.

[4]The distinction between automation and augmentation is increasingly central to the literature on AI deployment in organizations. For a useful framework, see Sebastian Raisch and Sebastian Krakowski, 'Artificial Intelligence and Management: The Automation-Augmentation Paradox,' Academy of Management Review 46, no. 1 (2021): 192–210.

# 11

# Designing for Formation

*How to deliberately recreate the conditions that build judgment—without sacrificing the genuine benefits of AI.*

There is a version of this chapter that begins with friction. That version argues that the efficiency era removed productive difficulty from organizational work, and that the response is to put some of it back—to reintroduce the friction that once formed judgment by forcing people to struggle with problems that the system has since learned to solve for them.

That version is not wrong, exactly. But it is imprecise in a way that matters. Because the goal was never friction. Friction was the mechanism. The goal was formation—the accumulated, contextual, consequence-tested understanding that, over time, becomes the judgment that organizations depend on. Friction produced formation because it connected people to real decisions, real consequences, and real relationships. Remove the friction and you remove those connections. Recreate the friction without recreating the connections, and you get something that feels like difficulty without actually developing anything.

The design challenge of this chapter is more specific than reintroducing friction. It is recreating the three conditions that friction historically made possible: authority that is real rather than ceremonial, memory that connects decisions to their consequences over time, and coordination that is distributed across the organization rather than concentrated at the top. These are the conditions under which judgment has always formed. And they are the conditions that three decades of automation—and now AI—have most systematically dismantled.

None of them require a retreat from AI. They require something more demanding: a conscious decision about how AI is deployed, and who retains genuine responsibility for what.

## The Ceremony of Control

There is a pattern that has become familiar in organizations that have deployed AI at scale, and it is worth naming precisely because it looks, from the outside, like exactly the right response to the concerns raised in this book.

The pattern works like this. An AI system generates an output—a recommendation, a draft, an analysis, a decision. A human reviews it. The human approves it. The output proceeds. From a governance standpoint, the loop appears closed. A person was present. A person approved. If anything goes wrong, there is a human being who is nominally accountable.

What this pattern obscures is the difference between nominal accountability and genuine authority. The human in that loop is, in most cases, not making a decision. They are performing a review of a recommendation that was generated by a system they do not fully understand, on the basis of context they did not assemble, toward an outcome the system has already effectively determined. Their presence is real. Their authority is not. They are, in the terms of this book's argument, a speed bump rather than a decision-maker.[1]

This is not a small distinction. The entire formation argument of this book rests on the claim that judgment is built through the experience of making decisions, observing their consequences, and carrying the learning forward. A person who is present at a decision without genuinely owning it is not accumulating judgment. They are accumulating the habit of deference—to the system, to the recommendation, to the authority that lives inside the model rather than in themselves.

The design challenge, then, is not how to keep humans in the loop. It is how to keep humans genuinely in authority—which is a more precise, more demanding, and more consequential standard.

What does real authority look like in an AI-augmented workflow? It has three properties. First, the person understands the context sufficiently to be able to challenge the AI's output rather than merely confirm it. Second, the person bears a genuine consequence—career, relational, reputational—for the quality of the decision, not just its formal approval. Third, the person carries forward, into the next decision, something that they learned from this one.

The third property is the one most frequently absent. And it is the one that matters most for formation.

## The Organizational Amnesia Problem

There is a phenomenon in modern organizations that has no commonly agreed name, but that every experienced leader will recognize immediately. It is the moment when you realize that the institution you are leading has stopped being able to learn from its own decisions.

It is not that mistakes aren't noticed. They are noticed. It is not that analyses aren't conducted. They are conducted, often extensively. It is that the learning extracted from those analyses does not change the way the next decision is made, because the people who made the original decision are no longer in the positions where the learning would apply, and the system that recorded the outcome does not carry the reasoning that produced it. The organization goes around the same loop, three years later, with a new cast, and arrives at a different conclusion for reasons that nobody present can quite articulate.

This is what organizational memory failure looks like in practice. And it is, at its core, a formation failure. Because the mechanism by which organizations learn—the mechanism by which the judgment of today's senior leaders becomes accessible to tomorrow's—is precisely the chain of decision, consequence, and visible reasoning that connects one generation of practitioners to the next.[2]

AI has accelerated this failure in a specific and underappreciated way. When an AI system produces an output—a forecast, a recommendation, a risk assessment—the reasoning that generated that output is largely invisible. The model processed patterns across vast quantities of data and arrived at a conclusion. What it cannot do, in any practically useful sense, is explain the reasoning behind that conclusion in a way that a junior professional can observe, internalize, and carry forward. The conclusion is available. The judgment that produced it is not.

This matters enormously for formation. In the old apprenticeship chain, a junior analyst did not just see the answer their senior colleague arrived at. They saw the process by which that colleague weighed the variables, questioned the assumptions, and made the call. That process was the curriculum. The answer was almost incidental.

The design question, therefore, is: how does an organization maintain the visibility of reasoning in an environment where a large and growing proportion of the analytical work is being done by systems that cannot make their reasoning legible?

Part of the answer is structural. Organizations can deliberately create the conditions under which the human reasoning around AI outputs remains visible and accumulated—the moments where experienced practitioners explain why they accepted a recommendation, why they challenged one, and what they were looking for that the system may not have been looking for. These moments are the new curriculum. They are not automatic. They require deliberate design. But they are possible, and they are the primary site where formation happens in an AI-augmented environment.

## The End-to-End Formation Path

Here is the central design principle of this chapter, and it is worth stating it plainly before working through its implications.

For most of the efficiency era, expertise was built within the sub-function. A finance professional learned accounts receivable. A logistics professional learned demand planning. A procurement specialist learned vendor negotiation. The unit of expertise was the functional silo, and progression within that silo was the model of career development. You went deeper into accounts receivable before you were given responsibility for the broader order-to-cash cycle, and you mastered that cycle before you were given any meaningful exposure to how cash flow connected to capital allocation decisions.

This model of formation had a logic to it—the logic of the efficiency era, which valued deep specialization and rewarded process mastery. But even within that logic, the formation that actually produced senior judgment was not the deep specialization. It was what happened when a professional had enough breadth of experience to begin seeing across the silos—to understand that the revenue forecast was not just a finance artifact, but the downstream consequence of commercial decisions made three months earlier; that the working capital number was not just a treasury concern, but the accumulated result of ten thousand operational choices happening across procurement, logistics, and sales.

The professionals who developed that cross-silo perspective were the ones who eventually became capable of the judgment that organizations depend on at senior levels. And they developed it, in the old system, largely by accident— by spending long enough in enough different parts of the organization that the connections eventually became visible.

AI has made the specialized sub-function largely redundant. The tasks that defined functional expertise—the reconciliations, the reports, the analyses, the forecasts—are now performed by systems, faster and more accurately than any human team could perform them. What AI cannot do is understand the flow: the sequence of dependencies through which an output in one part of the organization becomes the input for the next, and the human relationships that govern the quality of those handoffs.

This is where formation must now be deliberately concentrated.

Instead of developing expertise in the sub-function, the formation path of the future runs along the flow. A finance professional does not need to master the mechanics of account reconciliation. They need to understand why reconciliation matters—which relationships it implicates, what the consequences of a persistent discrepancy are, who in the commercial organization is affected when the numbers don't close, and what the conversation with those people needs to accomplish. And then they need to understand how that conversation connects to the next step in the flow: the working capital decisions that follow, the reporting that depends on accurate reconciliation, the business decisions made six months later that nobody will trace back to a conversation that happened in the finance function today.[3]

This is a fundamentally different unit of expertise. Not process knowledge— that now belongs to the system. Relational and contextual knowledge: the understanding of what each output in the flow means for the people who depend on it downstream, and the capability to manage those relationships across the entire chain.

The formation path, on this model, runs not up the silo but along the flow. A junior professional begins with one or two handoffs in a function—not mastering the mechanics of each, but understanding the purpose, the consequence, and the relationship. Over time, the range of that understanding expands: first within the function, then across the boundaries into adjacent functions, then outward into the business itself. The formation that results is not the deep specialization of the efficiency era. It is something more valuable and considerably harder to develop: an end-to-end understanding of how the organization actually works, held in a person rather than in a system.

This understanding—contextual, relational, accumulated along the flow—is precisely what AI cannot replicate. A system can track every handoff in the order-to-cash cycle. It cannot understand what is at stake in the relationship between the finance function and the commercial team when a difficult conversation about forecasting accuracy needs to happen. It cannot carry the history of that relationship, the trust that has been built or damaged, the unspoken dynamics that will determine whether the conversation produces alignment or defensiveness. That understanding is human, and it is developed only through the kind of accumulated relational exposure that the end-to-end formation path deliberately creates.

## From Orchestra to Ensemble

Chapter 10 introduced the idea of the formation-first leader—the person who creates the conditions in which judgment can develop in the people around them. The orchestra metaphor appeared there, and it is worth extending it here, because it contains a design principle that goes beyond leadership posture.

The metaphor, in its standard form, is this: the leader is the conductor, and the job of the conductor is to coordinate the ensemble. Individual musicians play their parts; the conductor holds the whole. Without the conductor, the performance degrades into noise.

This is the right image for what Chapter 10 is describing. But as a model for organizational design, it is insufficient. Because in a real orchestra, the conductor is not the only source of coordination. Every musician in the ensemble is listening continuously to every other musician—adjusting tempo, dynamics, and phrasing in real time in response to what they hear from their section and from the hall. The coordination is distributed. The awareness is mutual. A great chamber ensemble—a string quartet, say—has no conductor at all. The musicians coordinate entirely through their attentiveness to each other, through a shared understanding of the score so deep that they can anticipate each other's choices and respond before the note has been played.

The design implication for organizations is significant. A formation model that depends entirely on the leader to coordinate will break down whenever the leader is absent, changes, or fails to develop the capability described in Chapter 10. A formation model that distributes coordination across the organization—that makes every professional responsible for their attentiveness to the flow, to the people upstream and downstream from their position—is more robust, more scalable, and, crucially, more developmental. Because the act of listening across the ensemble is itself formation. It requires the kind of contextual awareness, relational intelligence, and systemic thinking that the end-to-end formation path is designed to develop.[4]

This is not a cultural aspiration. It is an organizational design question. The structures that make distributed coordination possible—the moments where people across functions, levels, and domains are in genuine dialogue about what is happening in the flow, not just reporting their piece of it upward—do not emerge naturally in organizations that have been optimized for efficiency. Efficiency-optimized organizations route coordination through formal channels: the weekly report, the monthly review, the escalation path. These channels are effective for transmitting information. They are not effective for developing the shared understanding of context and consequence that distributed coordination requires.

The design intervention is to create lateral permeability: the deliberate opening of channels through which people at different points in the flow are in regular, informal, genuine contact. Not briefings. Not status updates. Conversations about purpose, consequence, and context—the kind of conversations that allow a professional in one part of the flow to understand what their output actually means for the person at the next step, and to carry that understanding into how they do their work.

In an AI-augmented environment, these conversations become the primary site of formation. The system handles the mechanics. The human handles the meaning. And the meaning—what this output matters for, why that relationship is in tension, what the downstream consequence of this decision will be—is transmitted not through documentation or formal process but through the kind of ongoing lateral conversation that efficient organizations have been systematically eliminating for thirty years.

## The Signal That Makes It Real

All of this is, in the end, a cultural argument as well as a structural one. And cultural arguments have a well-known failure mode: they remain at the level of aspiration without ever changing the way decisions are actually made.

The reason they fail is usually not a lack of conviction. It is a lack of consequence. An organization can articulate a formation-first culture with genuine sincerity, can train its leaders in the principles, can publish the values and mean every word of them—and still find, five years later, that the dominant behavior in the organization is exactly what it was before. Because the dominant behavior is not shaped by what the organization says it values. It is shaped by what the organization actually rewards.

This is not a cynical observation. It is a structural one. Organizations are systems of incentives, and systems of incentives produce the behaviors they reward, regardless of what the culture deck says. If the organization rewards efficiency—if the people who get promoted are the ones who delivered the number, hit the target, and closed the quarter—then efficiency will be the dominant value, even in an organization that sincerely believes it values formation.

The design question, therefore, is not how to articulate the formation-first culture. It is how to make formation consequential—how to embed it into the reward structures, the progression criteria, the performance conversations, and the promotion decisions that actually shape what professionals in the organization believe matters.

There is a version of this that goes wrong, and it is worth naming. An organization can mandate formation-first behavior through the same rewards-and-consequences logic that has always driven efficiency-first behavior. These interventions are not without value. But they carry a risk that is structurally identical to the risk they are trying to address: that the behavior they produce is performance rather than genuine development. That professionals learn to demonstrate cross-functional awareness without actually developing it. That the measure becomes the goal, and the goal—formation—recedes.

The sustainable version of this signal is more demanding. It requires leaders who can distinguish, in the moment of a promotion or a performance conversation, between demonstrated capability and performed capability. Between the professional who has genuinely developed the end-to-end relational understanding that the formation path is meant to produce, and the one who has learned to produce evidence of it. That distinction is itself a judgment call—and it can only be made by leaders who have the formation to see it.

This is the recursive quality of the formation-first organization: it can only be built and maintained by people who have themselves been formed.

The leaders who can make the judgment call that distinguishes genuine development from its performance are, by definition, people whose own formation produced the contextual sensitivity to see the difference. They are the people who carry the apprenticeship chain in their own experience and who understand, from the inside, what it felt like to actually develop rather than simply advance.

The design implication is uncomfortable but important: organizations cannot shortcut the transition. They cannot simply mandate formation-first culture and expect it to materialize. They have to start with the people they have who are most formed—who carry the most contextual, relational, end-to-end understanding—and give those people the responsibility and the latitude to model the thing that the organization needs to become. Not as trainers. Not as mentors in the formal sense. But as the practitioners of a way of working that others can observe, absorb, and gradually make their own.

This is, in structural terms, the reconstruction of the apprenticeship chain. Not through the accidental proximity that produced it in the past, but through deliberate design: the creation of conditions under which the judgment held by the most formed people in the organization is visible, transmissible, and consequential for the people who are still developing it.

## What the Design Actually Looks Like

Principles without practice are philosophy, as Chapter 10 observed. So it is worth translating the three conditions of this chapter—real authority, consequence-linked memory, distributed coordination—into the texture of operational decisions.

Real authority, in practice, means asking a specific question before deploying AI in any workflow that involves consequential decisions: does the human who reviews this output have enough context to challenge it? Not in theory—

in practice, today, given what they actually know. If the answer is no, then adding a human review step does not create authority. It creates the appearance of authority while the effective decision remains inside the system. The design response is not to eliminate the AI step. It is to ensure that the human who engages with the output has been developed, through the end-to-end formation path, to the point where their engagement is genuine. This takes time, and it requires a formation investment that predates the workflow deployment. It cannot be retrofitted after the fact.

Consequence-linked memory, in practice, means designing the formation path to run through decisions—not past them. A professional who is developing along the end-to-end flow needs to be present not just when the output is produced but when the consequence of that output becomes visible, potentially months later. The account reconciliation conversation, the discrepancy that surfaces and gets resolved, the downstream impact on the commercial relationship—all of this needs to be part of the formation experience of the professional who initiated the process. Organizations that separate execution from consequence—assigning people to tasks without connecting them to the outcomes of those tasks—are not developing formation. They are producing sophisticated task-completers.

Distributed coordination, in practice, means protecting the lateral conversations that efficiency logic systematically eliminates. The informal exchange between the finance professional and the commercial lead that clarifies what the forecast is really based on. The cross-functional conversation between operations and procurement that surfaces why a vendor relationship is under strain. The moment in a project where someone from a different part of the organization asks a question that reframes the problem and changes the direction of the work. None of these are expensive. None of them require significant resources or structural change. They require, above all, permission—the signal from leadership that this kind of lateral engagement is valued, and that the time it takes is an investment rather than an inefficiency.

That signal—and the structures that make it credible—is the design work of the formation-first organization.

## The Efficiency Question, Answered

It is worth returning, at the close of this chapter, to the tension in its subtitle. Designing for formation without sacrificing the genuine benefits of AI.

The argument of this chapter is that this tension, examined carefully, dissolves. The genuine benefits of AI—the speed, the analytical horsepower, the capacity to process and synthesize at scales no human team could approach—are fully compatible with the formation conditions this chapter describes. In fact, they depend on them.

An AI system that processes the entire accounts receivable function with no human involvement produces efficiency. An AI system that processes the accounts receivable function while the human team develops end-to-end relational expertise, maintains genuine authority over consequential decisions, and uses the time freed by automation to deepen their understanding of the flow—that system produces efficiency and formation. The two are not in competition. They require different design choices, and they require leaders who understand that the purpose of the freed time is not to do more of the same work faster, but to do the work that the system cannot do: building the contextual, relational, consequence-tested understanding that will eventually become the judgment the organization depends on.

The organizations that will navigate the next decade well are not the ones that automate the most. They are the ones that use automation to free up the human capacity that can then be invested in the conditions under which humans genuinely develop. They are building something that no efficiency program has ever set out to build, and that no AI system can replicate: an organization that gets better at becoming, rather than simply better at doing what it already knows.

That distinction—between an organization that performs and one that compounds—is the subject of the final chapter.

## Notes

[1] The distinction between nominal and genuine authority in human oversight of AI systems is receiving increasing attention in the governance literature. For a rigorous treatment, see Inioluwa Deborah Raji et al., 'Closing the AI Accountability Gap: Defining an End-to-End Framework for Internal Algorithmic Auditing,' in Proceedings of the ACM Conference on Fairness, Accountability, and Transparency (2020). The concept of 'meaningful human control' over automated systems is developed more fully in Filippo Santoni de Sio and Jeroen van den Hoven, 'Meaningful Human Control over Autonomous Systems: A Philosophical Account,' Frontiers in Robotics and AI 5 (2018).

[2] The concept of organizational memory and its failure modes is explored in James G. March and Johan P. Olsen, Ambiguity and Choice in Organizations (Bergen: Universitetsforlaget, 1976), and more recently in James P. Walsh and Gerardo Rivera Ungson, 'Organizational Memory,' Academy of Management Review 16, no. 1 (1991): 57–91. The specific failure mode described here—the disconnection of decision reasoning from outcome tracking—is a consequence of the stateless architecture of most current AI systems, which produce outputs without preserving the reasoning chain that generated them.

[3] The argument for end-to-end expertise over functional specialization has a structural parallel in the operations literature on value stream mapping, developed from Taiichi Ohno's original insights in the Toyota Production System. See Taiichi Ohno, Toyota Production System: Beyond Large-Scale Production (Cambridge, MA: Productivity Press, 1988). The formation argument here is distinct, however: the goal is not process efficiency but relational and contextual development along the value chain.

[4] The distributed coordination model draws on research into high-reliability organizations. Karl E. Weick and Kathleen M. Sutcliffe, Managing the Unexpected: Sustained Performance in a Complex World, 3rd ed.

(Hoboken, NJ: Wiley, 2015), identify 'sensitivity to operations'—the distributed situational awareness across an organization—as a defining characteristic of these systems. The parallel to formation is direct: sensitivity to operations is not a property of the system; it is a property of the people inside it, developed through the kind of lateral attentiveness this chapter describes.

# 12

# The Adaptable Organization

*What the organizational model looks like when it is built for continuous becoming rather than stable execution.*

There is a question buried inside everything this book has been arguing, and it has not yet been asked directly. It is not a strategic question, and it is not a design question. It is an anthropological one.

The question is this: when intelligence becomes abundant — when analysis, synthesis, pattern recognition, and recommendation can be generated at scale and speed by systems that never tire and never forget — what remains specifically, irreducibly human?

The answer this book has been building toward is not creativity, though creativity matters. It is not empathy, though empathy matters. It is not even judgment, though judgment is the word the book has used throughout to describe what is at stake.

The answer is ownership.

Humans remain essential — to organizations, to institutions, to the systems through which societies coordinate themselves — precisely where decisions must be contextual, responsibility must be explicit, trade-offs must be owned, and consequences must be carried. AI can propose. AI can optimize. AI can execute with a speed and consistency no human team can match. But AI cannot be responsible. And the organizations, institutions, and societies that forget this distinction — that allow responsibility to become diffuse, accountability to blur, and the connection between decision and consequence to dissolve — are not becoming more efficient. They are becoming fragile in a way that does not show up in dashboards, and does not declare itself until something goes genuinely wrong.

This is the civilizational dimension of the argument that this book has been making at the organizational level. The judgment vacuum is not only an organizational risk. It is a symptom of a broader drift: toward systems in which intelligence multiplies faster than coordination, capability scales faster than accountability, and humans find themselves increasingly present but decreasingly responsible. The organizations that reverse that drift — that are designed, from the ground up, to keep responsibility explicit, memory alive, and human formation continuous — are not just better organizations. They are the template for how the AI era can be navigated without losing the thing that makes human institutions worth preserving.

The preceding two chapters described the leader and the design conditions that make this possible. This chapter describes the organization itself: what it looks like when those conditions are structurally embedded, what it feels like to work inside it, and what it takes to build it from where most organizations are right now.

## The Structural Shift

Every major technology wave has required organizations to restructure — not just adopt new tools, but reorganize around a different logic. The industrial era organized around function: the work was divided into specialisms and the specialisms were coordinated through hierarchy. The efficiency era organized around process: the work was re engineered into defined flows, and those flows were optimized and, increasingly, automated. Both models were rational responses to the conditions that produced them. Both created organizations that were well-adapted to stability — environments in which the primary challenge was executing a known playbook as reliably and cheaply as possible.[1]

The AI era presents a different challenge. Its defining feature is not the complexity of individual decisions — AI handles that better than humans. It is the pace at which the conditions that decisions are made under change. The environment in which the next generation of organizations will operate is not a complicated problem to be optimized. It is a continuously shifting context that must be continuously read — and read correctly, with the kind of contextual sensitivity that no system trained on historical patterns can reliably provide.

The organizational model that adapts to this challenge is not the functional hierarchy and it is not the re-engineered process. It is something closer to what a flowing system looks like when the people inside it understand the whole, not just their part. An organization structured not around what each function owns, but around how value moves: how the organization earns and how it invests, what flows in and what flows out, who depends on whom, and what the quality of every hand-off means for the person at the next step in the chain.

This is not an abstract redesign. Consider what it means in practice for a large organization. Instead of a finance function subdivided into accounts receivable, treasury, controlling, management accounting, and financial reporting — each with its own leadership, its own incentives, and its own version of what success looks like — imagine those activities organized around the flow of value they collectively serve. On one side of the organization, everything connected to how value is created and captured:

the commercial relationships, the revenue flows, the customer commitments that make the enterprise possible. On the other side, everything connected to how that value is deployed and sustained: the investment decisions, the operational costs, the capital allocation choices that determine what the organization becomes. In the middle, the people who sit at the hand-offs — who understand not just what their part of the process produces but what it means for the person who depends on it next, and the person after that.

What this structure changes is not primarily the process. The underlying activities are substantially the same. What changes is the unit of expertise — the answer to the question of what a professional in this organization is developing toward. Not mastery of a sub-function. Mastery of a flow. Not depth in accounts receivable, but understanding of why accounts receivable matters for working capital, why working capital matters for investment capacity, and why investment capacity matters for the commercial decisions being made on the other side of the organization. The expertise is end-to-end, relational, contextual — and it is, structurally, the kind of expertise that cannot be automated, because it lives in the person who holds it and nowhere else.

The adaptable organization is structured this way not because it is philosophically preferable. It is structured this way because it is the organizational form that generates, continuously and as a natural consequence of how work is organized, the judgment that the AI era requires.

## What Accumulates

There is a difference between an organization that performs and one that compounds, and the difference is not visible in the performance data for any given period.[2]

The performing organization delivers. It has strong execution, reliable processes, and good results — results that are largely explained by the quality of its systems and the discipline of its management. It is well-run, and it will continue to be well-run as long as the environment remains close enough to the one its systems were designed for. Its primary asset is its operating model, and its operating model is, in its essential structure, replicable. A competitor with sufficient capital and access to the same technology can, in time, build something similar.

The compounding organization is different in one specific way. What it accumulates, over time, is not better systems. It is better people — in the precise sense that the people inside it are, continuously, developing the contextual understanding, the relational intelligence, and the judgment that makes the organization capable of navigating conditions it has never faced before. When the environment shifts in ways the playbook did not anticipate, the compounding organization has something the performing organization does not: people whose formation has prepared them to read what is actually happening, rather than defaulting to what the system recommends.

This accumulation is not captured in any standard measure of organizational capability. It does not appear on a balance sheet. It is not tracked in a talent management system. It shows up only in the quality of decisions made under genuine novelty — in the moments when the data is ambiguous, the precedent is inapplicable, and the system's confidence is precisely the thing that should not be trusted. In those moments, the compounding organization has a resource that its competitors cannot buy and cannot quickly build: the accumulated judgment of people who have been genuinely formed.

The evidence that an organization is compounding rather than merely performing is not a number. It is a pattern of decisions. It is the fact that when the organization faces something genuinely new — a market shift that the models did not predict, a client relationship under unexpected strain, a strategic choice for which there is no comparable historical case — the people in the room can navigate it. Not because they have the right algorithm, but because they have the right formation. Because the organization has, over time, been building something in its people that is more durable than any system: the capacity to think well under conditions of genuine uncertainty.

This is what organizations are actually competing on in the AI era, whether they know it yet or not. And it is what the adaptable organization is designed to produce.

# The Operating Architecture

The adaptable organization is not only a different structural model. It runs on a different operating logic — a different set of principles governing how humans and AI work together, and what each is responsible for.[3]

The efficiency-first operating model was built on a single organizing principle: remove human involvement wherever a system can do the work more reliably and cheaply. This principle was rational under the conditions that produced it, and the efficiency gains it delivered were real. Its hidden cost — which this book has traced across eleven chapters — was the dismantling of the conditions under which the next generation of leaders would have been formed.

The operating logic of the adaptable organization rests on a different principle, and the difference is precise: AI executes where execution is the point; humans own where ownership is the point. The distinction between execution and ownership is not a matter of task complexity or analytical sophistication. It is a matter of responsibility. Ownership is present wherever a decision requires contextual judgment, wherever the trade-off cannot be fully specified in advance, wherever the consequence will need to be carried by someone who understood what they were choosing. In those moments, a human being must not merely be present — they must be genuinely responsible, which means they must have enough formation to understand what they are choosing and enough authority to choose it.

This distinction has three structural implications for how the adaptable organization is designed and governed.

The first is that governance is embedded rather than bolted on. In the efficiency-first model, governance was a control layer added after the operating model was designed — policies, reviews, and oversight mechanisms layered onto processes that were not built with accountability in mind. In the adaptable organization, the question of who owns a decision is answered before the AI is deployed to assist with it, not after. The governance structure is part of the operating architecture, not a supplement to it. This is not primarily a compliance argument. It is a formation argument: the people who bear genuine responsibility for decisions are the people who are developing judgment by making them. Remove the responsibility from the human, and you remove the formation opportunity.

The second implication is that memory is treated as organizational infrastructure, not a technical feature. Organizations make decisions over time, with context, with precedent, and with cumulative risk. A human leader who has been in a role for five years carries, in their formation, the institutional memory of how a hundred decisions were made and what their consequences were. When that leader leaves, that memory leaves with them — which is precisely the dynamic this book described in the retirement of Elena, and in every succession crisis that has followed. The adaptable organization designs for memory continuity: not by documenting everything, which produces archives rather than knowledge, but by ensuring that the people who make decisions remain connected, over time, to the consequences of those decisions. Memory is not a record. It is the lived connection between a decision and its outcome, held in a person who carries it forward.

The third implication is that human intent remains the origin of action throughout the organization. This is the deepest non-negotiable of the adaptable organization's operating model. In the drift toward full automation, organizations progressively lose the connection between what they intend and what they execute — not through any single decision, but through the accumulation of small delegations, each of which seems rational in isolation, until the moment when the organization cannot clearly articulate why it is doing what it is doing, or who made that choice. The adaptable organization structures against this drift. It ensures that at every consequential point in the flow, a human being can answer: this is what we intended, this is what we chose, and this is why.

These three structural elements — embedded governance, memory as infrastructure, human intent as origin — are not idealistic additions to an otherwise efficient system. They are the architecture of organizational intelligence: the conditions under which the organization gets smarter over time, rather than simply more capable of executing what it already knows.

# Building from Here

The adaptable organization is not a greenfield design. Most of the leaders who have read this far are not starting from scratch. They are running organizations that were built for a different era, with structures, incentives, and cultures that reflect the logic of efficiency-first management. The question of how to move from here to there is, therefore, the most practically important question this chapter can address.

There is an irony in the answer, and it is a generous one. The efficiency era, for all the damage it did to the conditions of formation, also created something that turns out to be unexpectedly useful for the transition: it centralized. The shared service centers, the enterprise platforms, the data lakes, the standardized processes that efficiency-era transformation produced — all of these represent a consolidation of organizational infrastructure that makes the end-to-end structural model achievable in a way it would not have been two decades ago. The functional expertise may have been lost. The plumbing, as it were, is in place. The adaptable organization can be built on top of it.

The obstacle is not structural, then. It is human — and it is precisely the kind of human obstacle that cannot be solved by a better process or a smarter system. The transition from functional silo to flow-based organization requires every functional leader to loosen their grip on the thing that has defined their authority: the function itself. The finance leader who owns finance, the operations leader who owns operations, the commercial leader who owns commercial — these are not people who have failed. They are people who built their careers and their identities on a logic that made complete sense for the era that produced it. Asking them to reorganize around the flow is asking them to relinquish the very thing that their formation rewarded.

This is why Chapter 10's argument about the identity shift of the formation-first leader is not merely a leadership development point. It is a prerequisite for the organizational transition. The leaders who can navigate it are those who have come to understand that the output of their organization is not the highest expression of their capability, and that the growth of the people around them, and the adaptability of the system they are building, is. Those leaders exist in most organizations. They are not always the most senior people. They are often the people who have been quietly building something different inside the existing structure, because they saw the formation problem before it had a name.

The starting point, for a leader who wants to build the adaptable organization from inside an existing one, is not an announcement. It is a structural choice, made quietly and consequentially: the decision to make one part of the organization — one function, one team, one flow — the prototype. To organize it around the end-to-end logic rather than the functional silo. To give the people inside it genuine authority over consequential decisions. To ensure they see the consequences of those decisions, and carry the learning forward. To protect the lateral conversations that make distributed coordination possible. And then to make that prototype visible — to let other parts of the organization see what is being built, and what it produces, and draw their own conclusions.[4]

Organizations do not transform through mandate. They transform through demonstration. The leaders who build the adaptable organization will not do it by announcing a new structure. They will do it by making the new structure undeniably better — at developing people, at responding to novelty, at navigating the conditions that the existing model was not designed for. And then, when the demonstration is clear enough, the organization will follow.

## The Organization That Keeps Its Shape

Return, for a moment, to Elena.

She retired at the end of Chapter 5, and the book has been building, in every chapter since, toward the question her retirement poses. Not the question of what to do about Elena — that is already, for most organizations, too late. The question of what needs to be true about an organization so that when Elena leaves, the thing she carried does not leave with her. So that the formation she held — the relational intelligence, the contextual sensitivity, the accumulated understanding of how the organization actually works — is not a personal asset that walks out the door, but an institutional capacity that has been transmitting itself, continuously, to the people who will need to exercise it next.

The adaptable organization is the answer to that question. Not because it has found a way to retain Elena — people retire, careers end, and the human knowledge held in any individual will always be, in part, irreplaceable. But because it has been designed so that the conditions that produced Elena are not accidental. So that the end-to-end formation path, the genuine authority over consequential decisions, the consequence-linked memory, the lateral conversations across the flow — these are not outcomes of a particular era's working conditions, but structural features of the organization itself. Built in, not bolted on.

What makes an organization adaptable, in the deepest sense, is not its capacity to restructure quickly when the environment shifts. Structure can always be changed. What makes it adaptable is the quality of judgment distributed across the people inside it — the degree to which every person in a consequential role has been genuinely formed, and is continuing to be formed, by the conditions in which they work. An organization in which that formation is continuous and structural has something that no efficiency program has ever delivered and no AI deployment can substitute: the capacity to encounter genuinely new conditions and navigate them well, not because the playbook covers it, but because the people can read it.

This is what it feels like, from the inside, to work in the adaptable organization. Not comfortable, exactly — the conditions for genuine formation have never been comfortable. But purposeful. Connected. The work has consequence that is visible rather than abstracted. The relationships are real rather than instrumental. The decisions belong to the people who make them, which means the learning belongs to them too. The system handles what the system handles, and the humans handle what the humans handle, and the difference between those two categories is understood rather than assumed. There is, in such an organization, a quality that is hard to name but unmistakable when you have experienced it: the sense that the people around you are actually developing — that they are, in the language this book has used throughout, becoming.

That quality is not produced by the right culture statement or the right leadership training program. It is produced by design: by the deliberate, structural choice to build an organization in which the conditions for formation are as carefully managed as the conditions for efficiency. Where the question of what the AI should do is always asked alongside the question of what the human needs to own, and both questions are answered seriously.

# The Choice That Only Organizations Can Make

AI will not pause to allow organizations to make this transition. The models will continue to improve. The deployment pressure will continue to build. The competitive environment will continue to reward — in the short run — the organizations that automate the fastest, regardless of what that automation does to the formation of the people inside them.

The judgment vacuum will, therefore, deepen before it is addressed. The current generation of judgment-holders will retire. The organizations that have not yet begun the transition will find themselves in the scenario this book described — facing genuine complexity with people who are technically capable and experientially hollow, equipped with excellent systems and insufficient judgment to know when those systems should not be trusted. That scenario is not inevitable. But it is the default.

The organizations that avoid it will not be the ones that resisted AI. Resistance is not a strategy; it is a delay on a declining curve. The organizations that avoid it will be the ones that made a different choice about what AI is for: not the elimination of human involvement wherever possible, but the liberation of human capacity for the work that human formation makes possible — the relational, the contextual, the consequential. The organizations that use the efficiency that AI genuinely delivers to invest in the formation that only humans can develop, and only organizations can provide the conditions for.

There is nothing technically complex about this choice. It does not require a new technology platform or a restructuring program or a change management initiative. It requires something simpler and harder: the decision, made by the people who lead organizations, that the development of the human judgment inside them is as important as the performance the systems they run are delivering. That the organization they are building is not just well-run, but capable of becoming. That the people inside it are not just productive, but being formed.

Every major technological transition in history has produced, alongside its efficiency gains, a question that the technology itself cannot answer: a question about what humans are now for. The steam engine produced it. Electrification produced it. The computer produced it. Each time, the answer was eventually found — not in spite of the technology, but in a new understanding of the specific contribution that remained irreducibly human once the technology had taken what it could take.

AI produces the same question, more urgently than any predecessor, because it reaches further into the domain that humans have always considered most distinctively their own: the capacity to reason, to weigh, to judge. The answer this time is the same in structure as it has always been — humans remain essential where responsibility must be owned, where consequences must be carried, where the trade-off cannot be specified in advance — but it requires something that previous transitions did not: a deliberate design of the conditions under which that human capacity is developed, because the conditions that previously produced it by accident no longer exist.

The organizations that make that design choice are building something that the AI era makes both more urgent and more valuable than at any previous moment in organizational history. They are building the capacity for genuine human judgment, in an era when judgment is the scarcest and most consequential resource an organization can hold.

They are building, in a precise and non-metaphorical sense, the organizations that the next era requires.

The question is simply whether enough of them will choose to do so before the last Elenas retire.

## Notes
[1]The concept of organizations adapting to technological change through

structural reorganization rather than mere tool adoption is explored in Alfred D. Chandler, Jr., Strategy and Structure: Chapters in the History of the Industrial Enterprise (Cambridge, MA: MIT Press, 1962). Chandler's core thesis — that structure follows strategy, and that major strategic shifts require corresponding structural transformation — applies with particular force to the AI transition, where the strategic imperative is a fundamental shift in the unit of organizational value.

[2] The distinction between organizations that perform and those that compound has a parallel in the finance literature on intangible capital. See Jonathan Haskel and Stian Westlake, Capitalism Without Capital: The Rise of the Intangible Economy (Princeton, NJ: Princeton University Press, 2017). Their argument that intangible assets — knowledge, relationships, organizational capability — are increasingly the dominant form of productive capital maps directly onto the formation argument: the compounding organization is one that is continuously building its intangible capital, rather than consuming it.

[3] The operating architecture described here — embedded governance, memory as infrastructure, human intent as origin — draws on the emerging literature on human-centered AI deployment and responsible AI governance. For a treatment of the costs when human accountability is removed from automated systems, see Virginia Eubanks, Automating Inequality: How High-Tech Tools Profile, Police, and Punish the Poor (New York: St. Martin's Press, 2018). The positive design case — what it looks like to embed human responsibility rather than remove it — is the contribution this architecture makes.

[4] The argument that organizations transform through demonstration rather than mandate draws on John P. Kotter, Leading Change (Boston: Harvard Business School Press, 1996), and his subsequent observation in Accelerate (Harvard Business Review Press, 2014) that the organizations best positioned for transformation maintain a dual operating system — a hierarchical structure for reliable execution alongside a more fluid network for adaptive change. The prototype logic described here is consistent with this model: building the new within the existing, until the new has demonstrated

sufficient advantage to lead.

* * *

# 13

# The Choice

*A direct address to the reader. This transition is survivable. It is even energizing. But it requires a decision that only humans can make.*

You are reading this at a particular moment in a transition that has no modern precedent. The tools available to you today can do things that were, five years ago, the exclusive province of skilled human practitioners. The tools available in five years will make today's seem primitive. This is not a cycle of incremental improvement. It is a structural shift in what intelligence means, how it is produced, and who — or what — produces it.

I have spent most of my professional life inside large organizations, helping them become more efficient. I know what that work felt like from the inside. I know the genuine satisfaction of watching a process that took forty people and six weeks become something that eight people could accomplish in three. I know the pride of delivering against a brief that, at the start of the engagement, seemed unreasonably ambitious. And I know — now, in retrospect, with the clarity that only distance provides — what we did not measure. What we did not even think to ask about. What we quietly removed from the system while we were busy improving it.

The junior analysts who no longer had to reconcile the accounts by hand.

The financial controllers who no longer had to build the models themselves. The strategy teams who no longer had to sit with raw data long enough to develop an instinct about what it was trying to tell them. I do not say this as a confession. I say it as a context for what follows, because the argument of this book has been built on an insider's authority — the authority of someone who delivered these transformations and has had long enough to watch what came after them.

What came after them was a generation of capable, intelligent, technically sophisticated professionals who were never given the conditions that produce judgment. Not because anyone decided to withhold those conditions. Because the conditions were removed by decisions that seemed, in the moment they were made, to be straightforwardly good.

That is the judgment vacuum. Not a failure of talent. A failure of conditions.

This book has made an argument. Let me state it plainly, one final time.

For most of modern organizational history, business judgment was produced by a system that nobody designed and that worked largely by accident. It was called experience. But underneath the word was a structure: a ladder of formation through which professionals moved, absorbing context through proximity, developing instinct through consequence, building the relational and situational understanding that eventually produced the judgment that organizations depend on. The ladder was imperfect. It was slow, inefficient, and often inequitable. But it worked, in the specific sense that mattered most: it produced people who could navigate genuinely novel conditions, read what the environment was actually telling them, and make decisions that no system could make on their behalf.

The efficiency era dismantled this system without intending to. It removed the entry-level work that had served as the organizational curriculum. It automated the variance that had been the formation mechanism. It offshored the transactional work that had, as its hidden function, transmitted the institutional memory of how an organization actually operated. And then AI arrived and reached further still — into the reasoning layer, the analytical layer, the very cognitive territory that previous automation had left intact.

The result is a vacuum forming at the base of every major organization. It is invisible today because the generation forged before automation is still in the room. When they leave — and they are leaving — the vacuum will become visible. Not as a dramatic collapse. As a drift. A slow, nearly imperceptible erosion in the quality of decisions made under conditions of genuine novelty. An organization that looks fine, by every conventional measure, and that is progressively less capable of reading what it cannot yet see.

That is the diagnosis. The book has been building toward a different destination.

The destination is not a warning. It is a design challenge. And it is solvable.

I want to be precise about what "solvable" means, because the word can carry more optimism than the situation warrants. The judgment vacuum cannot be solved by a training program, a mentoring scheme, or a well-intentioned leadership initiative. It cannot be solved by reducing AI adoption, or by redesigning job descriptions, or by any intervention that leaves the underlying conditions — the conditions under which judgment forms — unchanged.

It can be solved by organizations that are willing to treat human formation as a design constraint: as seriously as they treat efficiency, as deliberately as they approach technology deployment, as consequentially as they measure financial performance. Organizations that understand that the time AI frees up is not an invitation to do more of the same thing faster, but an opportunity to do the thing that AI cannot do — to invest that freed human capacity in the relational, contextual, consequence-bearing work through which judgment develops.

It can be solved by leaders who have made the identity shift described in Chapter 10: who have come to understand that their primary responsibility is not the performance of this quarter but the formation of the organization that will outlast them. Who have grasped that the most consequential thing they will build is not a system or a strategy or a set of results, but the judgment capacity of the people they are developing — the pipeline that does not yet exist and that they are the only ones positioned to create.

It can be solved by organizations that are willing to restructure around the flow of value rather than the logic of the silo, to embed governance in the operating model rather than bolt it on afterward, to treat institutional memory as infrastructure rather than archive, and to insist that human intent remains the origin of every consequential action the organization takes.

None of this is technologically complex. All of it is humanly demanding. The obstacle is not a capability gap. It is a choice.

Let me say something about that choice more directly than the chapters that preceded this page have done.

You are reading this, I assume, because you lead something, or aspire to lead something, or because you are trying to understand the environment in which you will spend the next several decades of your working life. The argument of this book was addressed, in the main, to the organizational and strategic dimensions of the problem. But the problem has a personal dimension too, and the epilogue is the place to name it.

There is a version of the next decade in which you navigate it as a consumer of AI capability. You use the tools well. You deploy them intelligently. You capture the efficiency gains and deliver strong results. You are good at your job, by every conventional measure, and you are recognized as such.

And at the end of that decade, if you are honest with yourself, you find that you are technically more capable than you were at the start of it — and contextually, relationally, judgmentally, not quite what you expected to become. Because the conditions that would have formed you were the conditions you optimized away.

There is another version. In this version, you decide — consciously, deliberately, against the path of least resistance — that the efficiency gains are a means and not an end. That the time AI frees up is formation time, and you treat it as such. That the decisions that come to your desk are not just problems to be resolved but opportunities to develop the people who will need to resolve them without you someday. That the organization you are building is not just well-run but capable of becoming — and that the distinction between those two things is the most important strategic insight available to you.

The second version is harder. It requires holding two things at once: the genuine benefits of AI, and the genuine irreplaceability of human judgment. It requires resisting the pressure — and the pressure is real, and it will not diminish — to let efficiency be the organizing principle of every decision. It requires the kind of leadership that Chapter 10 describes: not the leader who is accountable for the result, but the leader who is accountable for the conditions under which the next generation of results will be made.

It also, and I say this with the conviction of someone who has experienced both sides of it, produces something more sustaining than efficiency alone. The meetings described at the opening of Chapter 10 — the ones that feel alive rather than performed, where people arrive with genuine thinking and leave with something they did not have when they walked in — those meetings happen in organizations that are in the second version. Not always. Not easily. But they happen, and when they do, they produce something that no dashboard captures: the sense that what you are building is growing, rather than simply running.

That is not a soft observation. It is the most precise description I have of what organizational compounding feels like from the inside.

The transition is survivable. Every major technological transition has been survived, and most of them, in retrospect, produced conditions of human flourishing that were unimaginable at the moment of maximum anxiety about their consequences. The fear that electricity would make human physical labor worthless turned out to be misplaced. The fear that computers would make human analytical capability obsolete turned out to be misplaced. The human contribution shifted, and then found its new form, and the new form turned out to be more valuable, more interesting, and more distinctively human than what preceded it.

AI will not be different in this ultimate structure. The human contribution will shift. It will find its new form. And the new form — judgment, ownership, the irreducibly consequential — turns out already to be visible, in the organizations that are furthest ahead in navigating this transition. It is not a consolation prize. It is the actual prize: the work that is most demanding, most contextual, most resistant to substitution, and most aligned with the thing that makes human professional life worth investing in.

But — and this is the qualification that the optimistic reading of technological history tends to elide — the transition is not automatic. The shift from what humans used to do to what humans will do in an AI-augmented world does not happen on its own. It requires deliberate design of the conditions under which the new human contribution is developed. It requires organizations that treat formation as seriously as they treat efficiency. It requires leaders who understand that the most valuable thing they are building is not a system but the judgment inside the people who work with it.

That is the work. And it is energizing — genuinely, sustainably energizing — in a way that pure efficiency management has never been. Because it is the work of building something that grows.

The junior analyst from the opening of this book — the one who was sitting close to the raw materials of organizational life thirty years ago, absorbing context through proximity, learning to read the organization through its numbers — is now, if they have moved through the career that work prepared them for, somewhere near the top of a large organization. They are, in the language of this book, a judgment-holder.

They are also, in many cases, beginning to wonder who will carry what they carry when they leave.

The answer to that question is the one this book has been building toward. The judgment they carry was produced by conditions. Those conditions can be recreated — not accidentally, as they were when that analyst first sat down with the invoices and the reconciliations, but deliberately, structurally, by design. Not the same conditions: the work is different now, the tools are different now, and the formation path runs along the flow rather than up the silo. But conditions with the same essential properties: real authority, consequential memory, distributed coordination, and the understanding that what the organization is developing in its people is more durable and more valuable than anything the systems can produce on their behalf.

The choice to create those conditions is available to every leader reading this. It does not require a mandate from above or a restructuring approved by the board. It requires the decision to begin — in one team, one function, one carefully designed prototype — and to make that beginning visible enough that others can see what it produces.

That is how the transition becomes survivable. Not all at once, and not without difficulty, but through the accumulation of deliberate choices made by the people who have understood what is at stake and decided to act on that understanding.

You are one of those people now. The question is what you do next.